The
KINGDOM
IS YOURS

The
KINGDOM
IS YOURS

LOUIS H. EVANS

FLEMING H. REVELL COMPANY

WESTWOOD, N. J.

LOS ANGELES · LONDON · GLASGOW

Contents

The
KINGDOM
IS YOURS

Seek ye first the kingdom of God, and his righteousness; and all these things shall be added unto you.

MATTHEW *6:33*

Your Kingly Purpose

MAY I START WITH A RATHER PRESSING, IMPUDENT QUES-
tion? If there should suddenly come to you this clarion
query, "For what are you living—what comes first with
you?" would you have a quick, crisp, and decisive answer? What is the fundamental strategy underlying
your days—your life?

Someone has said that in war, mistakes in tactics,
a bad carrying out of detailed plans, may be forgiven,
but that no commanding officer is forgiven if he makes
a mistake in strategy, the general plan of large-scale
action. In this battle of life you and I may make individual mistakes, but we must not make mistakes in
strategy, in the general plan of our days.

In football a man may fumble a ball, even be
tackled for a loss, but there is no excuse for a man's
not knowing where the goal is or knowing what it is
to score.

God, through His son, Jesus Christ, has given us

life's supreme purpose. It is found in Matthew 6:33: "Seek ye first the kingdom of God, and his righteousness; and all these things shall be added unto you"— shall be as additions, as of secondary importance to you —but this is supreme!

There is the pressure of many other tempting goals. The Fascists said, "I seek first the State." The Nazis said, "I seek first the race." The Shintoist said, "I seek first the Emperor." The Communist says, "I seek first the society of one class." The hedonist says, "I seek first pleasure." The lover says, "I seek first love and affection." The physiologist says, "I seek first the health of my body." The mercenary man says, "I seek first wealth and possession." The tragedy is that any one of these things may easily become our god if it maneuvers itself into first place in our interests and in our vital service.

But across a frustrated world there comes this vitalizing, clarifying, thrilling command of Christ, "Seek ye first the kingdom of God, and his righteousness."

We pray easily, and sometimes unthinkingly, "Thy kingdom come." What do we mean by that? It is explained in the next verse, "Thy will be done on earth as it is in heaven." In building God's Kingdom here we strive merely to see that things are done on earth as they are in heaven.

Let us conduct an interesting personal experiment. Ask yourself, or someone else, this pointed question, "What is your vocation?" Undoubtedly you will receive replies like one of these, "Butcher," "Baker," "Candlestick maker," "Doctor," "Lawyer," "Indian Chief," "Parson," "Pugilist," "Housewife," "Athlete," "Astronomer." These occupations, however, are more a means of making a living than a description of what one is living for. We all have one great vocation. We are all called to this: "Seek ye first the kingdom of God and his righteousness." To this cause we are all born. That is the vocation of every man, woman and child. Now, our profession happens to be the particular tool we choose to bring that kingdom to pass, but the profession must be ever merely the "tool" of one's "vocation."

When we divorce one's profession from his vocation we begin to get into trouble. I remember that I was giving some addresses at a state university when a certain naval officer invited me to visit a great ordnance plant. I saw there the twelve- and fourteen-inch guns, enough electrical aiming and firing gadgets to rearm every ship in the Western navy. As I looked at those great death-dealing instruments, I said to him, "Captain, are you going to use these things some day?" He replied, "I don't think that is my business, Dr. Evans. That's up to you religionists." I said, "Wait a minute, sir. You can't pass the responsibility to me that way! Building a kingdom of peace and righteousness is as

much your task as it is mine." You see, he was so busy
with the profession of making guns that he forgot his
vocation of building a kingdom of righteousness and
peace. He had never thought out how his profession
might make its contribution to that. He was so busy
making a living he had forgotten what he was living
for.

The moment men of science divorce their instruments from their intentions, if we come to the day
when our scientific inventions are no longer captained
by our spiritual intentions—then civilization is on its
way out. This man thought he could sleep on Sunday
mornings and make guns during the week, while others
of us rose and got ourselves to the temple and to the
church to attend to our vocation—the chief end of all
men!

A high-school girl, with her hands in the greasy
dish water, while her loving mother was wiping the
dishes, said in utter disgust, "Mother, how do you
stand washing dishes year after year?" Her mother replied, "My dear, I am not washing dishes, I am building a home for God." You and I would very easily
walk out on some of these mundane tasks if this regal,
royal purpose did not crown even the seemingly mean-
est endeavor.

Queen Victoria said, "I am queen by the grace of
God." This was her way of serving Him. Roland
Hayes stood with closed eyes and folded hands before

he sang on the stage before the multitude, asking Christ to use his voice as a tool for something greater.

What was the platform that Jesus laid down for His Kingdom? He gave it in His inaugural address just after His baptism and His commissioning, in the synagogue at Nazareth, when He said, "The Spirit of the Lord is upon me, because he hath anointed me to . . ." (Luke iv) to do what? I have been baptized to what end? Here are the planks of His platform and His program: First, "to preach the gospel to the poor." Yes, our baptism must have something to do with the poor and their need of us. Second, "He hath sent me to heal the brokenhearted," and you and I must be the givers of comfort and strength. Third, "to preach deliverance to the captives." You and I must set this world free from every yoke and bondage of sin and captivity. Fourth, "and recovering of sight to the blind"; yes, we must see that too—the curing of man's spiritual and physical blindness. Fifth, "to set at liberty them that are bruised,"—to reach out today and help mankind recover from its wounds, physical, mental, and spiritual. Finally, "to preach the acceptable year of the Lord,"—to strive to build such an empire on earth as will be acceptable to God and His great pattern. Then Christ "closed the book" and "sat down."

My friends, you and I dare not close the book and sit down at the end of life until we have done these things.

The most vital religious experiences will have something to do with building this kind of a Kingdom. We will see how this is part of the purpose of the Cross, that we are saved to serve. We will see that this is part of the genius of our prayer life. The prayer chamber will become the briefing room for holy service. In our baptism, let us be sure that *cleansing* will always be followed by a *campaign* for Him. Our highest religious *experiences* must end in an *expedition* for God. Our truest *conversion* must partly manifest itself in *co-operation* with God. The best kind of *worship* will express itself in later *work,* and in our devotional life our deepest *communion* will always end in a *commission* to be utterly available to God and the things of His Kingdom.

You and I can make no greater contribution to the present situation than to "seek first the kingdom of God, and his righteousness," as we find them portrayed and demonstrated in Jesus Christ.

A great Italian critic and historian said, "Rome fell for three reasons: because the bank, the academy and the temple were against Jesus of Nazareth." And when in any nation the academy—its education, the temple—its religion, and the bank—its financial and economic system, are against the principles of Jesus of Nazareth, that nation, too, will fall!

Christ came to earth for a specific reason: to bring this world and humanity back to fellowship with God again. The world, this celestial ball, has rolled out of the garden of God's will. Christ came to bring it back and place it in the hand of God, and this is your holy task and mine—to help Him do just that.

John Bannister Tabb has given us the meaning of Christmas in a few lines:

> A little Boy, of Heavenly birth,
>   But far from home today,
> Comes down to find His ball, the earth,
>   That sin has cast away.
> O Comrades, let us one and all
>   Join in to get Him back His ball.*

That is your task and mine—to bring this world and civilization back to God. This is our royal partnership with Christ, this is the vital meaning of living. Without this we have merely existed, we have never lived. A blacksmith's bellows breathes, but it does not live; many of us breathe physically, but we are not alive spiritually to this great purpose of our day.

"But will these messages about the Kingdom of God have nothing to do with my personal problems— my tears, my fears, my tragedies and my cares?" you might ask. They will have everything to do with them. Those ills of life from which we suffer are but the rash that breaks out on the surface of our lives when the bloodstream of our purpose is poisoned or weak or

---

* *Masterpieces of Religious Verse,* Harpers, p. 695.

anemic. If we fail to "seek first the kingdom of God" —if things are wrong at the center of life—then things will be wrong at the circumference of life.

"But," you say, "my home is crashing in." A home, you know, is like a solar system. The thing that holds that system together is the fact that a great sun is in its center, without which it would fly to pieces. And unless the Son of God is put at the center of the home, any hearthside may fly to pieces. Have you united in marriage to serve Him? Then that home will likely stay together. While one home in every three in America is broken by divorce, only one out of every fifty-seven homes of church members goes to pieces. Why? Because at their center there is the sun, the Son of God!

"But," you say, "my child has gone wrong." Was there planted in his or her heart the royal purpose to serve God? Would you say honestly that this has been your most vital gift to him or her?

"But I live in fear of this atomic power and of death by an atomic explosion!" So do I! A scientist said to a college group some time ago, "If we do not learn to live together as Christian people within the next five years, we shall all have died together." Another scientist said, "The only defense against the atom bomb is spiritual defense." Are you and I honestly helping to build it?

"But do you realize my burden of taxes and

maintenance?" Certainly I do! But when we pour twenty-five times more into the military than we do into missions; when we pay fifty billion dollars a year to put guns in our hands and only two billion dollars a year to put spiritual goals in the hearts of men, then, of course, we will pay! General MacArthur said, "You cannot save the flesh until you save the spirit." *

When we spend as much on missionaries as we spend on brave Marines; when you and I give as much for brotherhood as for battleships; when we spend as much on Bibles as on bombs; when we are as alive to spread the Gospel of Christ as a Communist is to spread his cause; when we put first things first, then God will relieve us of this burden, and we will be on our way.

The trouble today is that we Americans have been giving ourselves to secondary things. "Seek ye first the kingdom of God, and its righteousness," but for many of us it has been far down the list, not even a bad second, and this royal purpose has not fared well. We Americans—a lot of us—have lost our sense of the vital!

William Hunt, a great artist, was coaching a class in landscape painting. It was in the late afternoon and he had suggested that they paint the sunset. As the sun was sinking below the horizon, he looked over the shoulder of one of his most promising art pupils and

* From MacArthur's speech on the battleship *Missouri* at the Japanese surrender.

noticed, to his dismay, that the young man, instead of painting the glorious sunset, had spent all his time painting an old red barn with decaying shingles. In alarm, the great artist and teacher exclaimed, "Son, son, it won't be light long! You haven't time for both shingles and sunsets. You must choose!" Let us not spend our days, our hours, our energies, our purses on painting old barns and shingles—the mundane earthly things of life—for it will not long be light. Rather, splash the sun, the spiritual things on the canvas of your life while it still is light. Then hope will rise above the destroyed cities and the scarred lands of this world with healing in its wings!

Quietly now, is this the purpose of your life, honestly to seek "first the kingdom of God, and his righteousness"? Then yours is the royal life. You are not merely existing, you are living!

Pilate therefore said unto him, Art thou a king then?
Jesus answered, Thou sayest that I am a king.

JOHN 18:37

Pilate saith, Behold your King!

JOHN 19:14

Ladies and Gentlemen, Meet the King!

IF IT IS REALLY TRUE THAT WHEN YOU AND I FACE JESUS
Christ in actuality, we face the King of the Universe—
then that is an arresting meeting! Part of the unique-
ness of Jesus Christ lies in His breath-taking claims.
Pilate said, "Art thou a King then?" Jesus replied,
"Thou sayest that I am a King." Pilate then said to
the crowd, "Behold, your King." Christ did not deny
it. He was ever speaking of "my kingdom." When He
rode into Jerusalem the people cried, "Behold, thy
King cometh, sitting on a colt," He accepted those
plaudits as their King. He made this startling state-
ment about the future, "Henceforth ye shall see the
Son of man sitting at the right hand of power, and
coming on the clouds of heaven." And in the end,
you and I are asked to believe that this cry will go up
along the spaces of Heaven, Rejoice, for "the kingdoms
of this world are become the kingdoms of our Lord
and of his Christ; and he shall reign for ever and

ever . . ." King of kings and Lord of lords! Hallelujah!

Those claims are certainly unique and arresting! Somehow, we cannot escape them. As Carnegie Simpson, in *The Fact of Christ,* said, "The fact of Christ is not just a fact of history; it has become, also, a fact of conscience. It has arrested and arraigned our moral being." If we honestly try to examine Jesus Christ intellectually before the tribunals of our minds, suddenly we find that the situation is reversed and He is examining us. We study famous persons such as Plato, Aristotle, and Philo, and in the realm of the mind we are sometimes elevated and enthralled, but when we study Jesus Christ we are spiritually upset and strangely disturbed. Who He is, suddenly resolves itself into what we should do with Him. We have no sooner asked the question, "What think ye of Christ?" than immediately we are led strongly to the position where we must say, "What shall I do with Him?" There is no one like Him in history. Every man stands face to face with His startling kingly claims.

Another thing that makes our relationship with this King unique is the possibility of fellowship with Him. Fellowship with kings is usually reserved for the few. To have audience with a queen has become an act of privilege, and it is always carefully prepared for and rehearsed. In the army it is unusual for a private to have audience with a general and he is fortunate if he even sees one.

But these privileges are daily practices with the followers of Christ. There is not a day when the Christian cannot have personal audience with Him in prayer—or should have. No man should ever join a church, which is the Army of Christ, without having known Him and met Him personally. More startling still, Christ never sends a man on an errand without the promise of going with him—"Lo, I am with you always, even unto the end of the world." As Alexander Maclaren said years ago:

The peculiarity of Christianity is the strong personal tie of real love and intimacy which will bind men, to the end of time, to this Man who died nineteen hundred years ago.

We look back into the wastes of antiquity and mighty names rise there which we reverence; there are great teachers from whom we have learned and to whom, after a fashion, we are grateful. But what a gulf there is between us and the best and noblest of them!

But there is nothing in the whole history of the world in the least like that strange bond which ties you and me to Jesus Christ.

We stretch out our hands across the waste, silent centuries, and there we touch the warm, throbbing heart of our Friend who lives forever and is ever near us.

A perpetual bond unites men with Christ today. And there are no limitations in that friendship, no misconstructions in that heart, no alienations possible, no changes to be feared. There is absolute rest for us there.

Why should I be solitary if Jesus Christ is my Friend?

Why should I fear if He walks by my side? Why should anything be burdensome if He lays it upon me and helps me to bear it? What is there in life that cannot be faced and borne—aye, and conquered—if we have Him, as we all may have Him, for the Friend and the home of our hearts? *

Of course, there are certain attitudes the heart and mind must assume before He becomes our King and we His true subjects. It is not natively true of us that we belong to this Kingdom of Faith originally and naturally.

Paul said, "Remember, that once ye were at that time separate from Christ, . . . and strangers from the covenants of the promise, having no hope and without God in the world. But now in Jesus Christ ye that once were far off are made nigh in the blood of Christ. So then ye are no more strangers and sojourners, but ye are fellow citizens with the saints and of the household of God."

Christ stands at the door and knocks, but if He enters He will come in only as a king. You must abdicate the throne of your will and allow Him to step up into this royal chair. You must be willing to say, "I have been crucified with Christ; yet I live; and yet no longer I, but Christ liveth in me." It will truly be Christ increasing while you are decreasing, you remaining silent when Christ is speaking, you becoming

* Alexander Maclaren, in *The Baptist Bulletin*.

less and less while Christ becomes more and more, until you are nothing and Christ is everything! This is the yielded and the kingly life.

When this naturalization into the Kingdom of God takes place, certain things come to pass in the yielded life of empire.

This will undoubtedly change our *prayer life*. We will realize, first of all, that we are in the presence of the King and who it is that gives us audience. A holy awe and reverence will seize our souls as we have careful speech with this King of kings.

Our prayers will have not only the personal aspect but a certain sweep of empire. Our hearts will not only putter around in the small areas of our own personal problems but will yield themselves to the great collective prospect of the world for Christ. We will no longer ask merely for things, we shall have outgrown that. A woman was asked, "What did you pray for today?" To which she replied, "Oh, I am passed that—just asking for things—I have taken the lid off my soul!" We shall spend much time talking about kingly things and not clutter up His royal room with selfish chatter; the heart will not only kneel to receive His blessing, it will also stand to receive His orders and our deepest communion with Him will be followed by definite commitments for service; we will not spend our time heaven-gazing alone; these times with the King will also lead to world-changing.

A greater conception of the presence of this King will also *give dignity to our worship* of Him, personal and collective. The founder of the Cistercian Order in England used to stand with his hand on the knob of the chapel door for several minutes before entering —he was a man of worldly cares and wanted to leave these behind when he came to talk to the King.

There will also be something tremendously cleansing about this presence. Isaiah said, when he entered into the temple, "I saw the Lord sitting upon a throne, high and lifted up; and his train filled the temple." Then he said, "Woe is me! for I am undone; because I am a man of unclean lips, and I dwell in the midst of a people of unclean lips: for mine eyes have seen the King." It takes courage to go to the sanctuary and worship. There is something courageously cleansing about it! A certain man said, "I do not go to church for three reasons. First of all, God does not make me; second, there is a great gulf between what I am and what I should be; and, finally, I do not want to be reminded of it." Three reasons sufficient to keep any man from the presence of God. Each time we see Him we become abased with humility, but receiving Him we have an elevated feeling of having reached up, having grown tall by walking with Him, and of, somehow, having started climbing again.

Again, the unique presence of this King stirs our lives and our spirits inevitably to helpful *service*. The early Christians, sensing His kingly presence, went out, "the Lord *working with them.*" Let us remind ourselves not merely that the Lord was "with them" but that the Lord was "*working* with them."

We have said before that communion always should end in commitment. Someone whispered to a man in a church sanctuary, "When does the service begin?" To which he replied, "The service begins when the meeting ends." The devotional chamber and the worship of God are but the briefing rooms from which we fly to our objectives. After worship we should be very impatient to get to work.

Commercialized athletics in the United States makes many spectators in the grandstand but not too many performers on the field. Likewise, we often commercialize our religion and farm it out to a few professional performers while we sit back in the grandstand, applauding or complaining of the progress of the great spiritual cosmic game or lack of it. We become backseat drivers, critical, impatient, often with hands that never touch the wheel. "It is no longer the Christian's chief temptation to want to occupy the chief seats in the synagogues; more likely we are tempted to sit in the rear seats and avoid our spiritual responsibility." We live in a day in which it is very easy to buy the ticket of privilege and deteriorate merely into the rôle of spectator. We have fallen prey to the sin of the "Cinema Mind." We watch a film or play, sometimes weep as though we were peeling an onion, forgetting that there is nothing as weepy as a block of ice, then often go out and do nothing!

It will never be enough for us to accept Christianity and its privileges as the King's men and women —we must give them out again. When Christ spoke to the woman of Samaria, evangelism to Him was not only making a Christian of her, He also made an evangelist of her and she ran to the village and cried, "Come, see a man which told me all things that ever I did: is not this the Christ? Then they went out of the city, and came unto him." If all the women of the royal household of God would talk about God like that—whole towns would come out to see Him. This is our obligation in the social strata. Teachers, too, have a wonderful opportunity in public schools and universities as well as in church schools. You who teach the sciences in an atomic age like this are as important as those who teach the Bible, Christian literature and religion. You in lay pursuits must redeem science and captain it with the human soul, add spirituality to smartness and love to these limbs of steel!

The kingliness of Jesus Christ also lays before you parents an unspeakable privilege. As the king passed in a procession in England a father lifted his boy on his shoulders, saying, "Son, I want you to *see* the king." There is no greater obligation, father and mother, than to lift your child on your shoulders in order that he may see the King in this day of tawdry purpose.

Once we are the wise subjects of this King we also suddenly share His *regal confidence* in the things of His empire. It is only natural, I suppose, that you and I should at times be disturbed by the colossal movements of Communism and paganism throughout this world. The struggle has largely resolved itself into two great forces, Communism and Christianity—Communism with man in the saddle and Christianity with God in the saddle. God, for some reason, has permitted spirituality and materialism to exist side by side and you and I cannot escape this conflict. It is not enough that you and I be free from personal worries, that our minds and hearts be cleansed of various personal complexes and "phobias" of life, until we become tremendously sorry for ourselves. We do not come into the harbor of the Church and the Kingdom ready merely to have our tattered sails mended, the hulls of the ships of our personalities repaired, and our holds stocked with precious hopes. This is, of course, a part of the Christian process and I would not underestimate it, but our chief aim for coming into the Kingdom of God and into the Church is to arm ourselves for future struggle—to seek first the Kingdom of God; the harbor of the spiritualities is to rearm ourselves for the holy warfare and to sail out conquering and to conquer. Thus we save ourselves from allowing Christianity to become merely an escapism; we remember that we are "saved to serve," and our faith is suddenly married forever to the holy, brave warfare.

Yes, it looked bad for Christ when He stood before Pilate with His hands bound with the hempen cords of hatred, but across that courtroom of Roman satellites there boomed these words from His royal lips, "My kingdom!" They said when they saw the boldness of Peter and John that they had "been with Jesus," and His kingly courage became theirs. Yes, it looked bad when Paul stood before Nero. The Roman legions were arrayed against him. It seemed then that the empire of Christ had not a single chance. But nineteen hundred years have passed since then and Cæsar is dead, as dead as men can be, but Paul is very much alive in the hearts of many, and today, you call your son, "Paul," but you call your poodle-dog "Cæsar." And it will happen again! This kingly Christ has unhorsed every dictator who ever marched against Him, and every one of them will bite the dust, and of His kingdom there shall be no end!

Remember, my friends, when you rivet your life and your faith and the force of your personality to the Kingdom of God and to this kingly Christ, you give obeisance and pay homage and proffer your life to Someone who is unending, unimpeachable, undefeatable in the ranks of time! We invite you to this Kingdom, to the royal life which is in Jesus Christ our Lord.

For thou wast slain, and didst purchase unto God with thy blood men of every tribe, and tongue, and people, and nation, and madest them to be unto our God a kingdom and priests; and they reign upon the earth.

REVELATION 5:9, 10

The Kingly Purchase

To whom do you and i belong? deep in everyone's heart someone, something wears a "crown." In a study of history it would be of more than passing interest to make a study of how kings came to own their subjects or to rule over them. We would find that some conquered the people by force, others by propaganda and enslavement of the people's minds, still others by intrigue. Christ came to His mastery by a loving purchase and, at least, this will be a part of the picture.

One of the reasons for this kingly ransom is found in our text. Before we mention this claim of God upon us, we might mention the other rights by which our personalities should belong to Him. We are His, of course, by right of *creation*. The words, "In the beginning God . . ." are an explanation of your life and mine. We are His by right of His sovereign creatorship. Again, we are His because of His daily *sustaining*. He is the Lord of life, and life is His gift. Our days are allotted to us by Him who is our daily Sustainer.

Finally, we are His by the right of His loving purchase. In Revelation 5:9 we find these arresting words: "Thou didst purchase unto God with thy blood men of every tribe, and tongue, and people, and nation, and madest them to be unto our God kings and priests; and they reign upon the earth."

How did we come upon this regal standing which we have with God? How did we become a part of this kingdom? The Greek word here for "purchase" is *agoradzo*. The true meaning of this word will bring us to the Grecian, Roman or Oriental market place as it functioned in the time of Christ. Here on the selling block stood men who were sold for debts they were unable to pay; because they were hopelessly in debt their freedom had been forfeited. The highest bidder purchased such a person as a *doulos* or slave, to be his own altogether and to serve him forever.

This was your condition and mine spiritually; we were "sold under sin." Spiritual debts had mortgaged our souls beyond any possibility of our paying or making remission for them. We had lost our spiritual right to freedom. Justice would decide that and preside over the merits or demerits of our lives. Suddenly God's Son offers Himself: "I give my life a ransom." The Kingly One, by every right of this purchase, may step forward and claim us for His own. From that moment on, if we accepted the purchase, we became His—every atom of our being, every fiber of our mind and muscle, every ability of our lives. We became His "redeemed ones," his *douloi,* slaves of God, the servants of Christ!

Paul reminds us of this when he says, "Ye are not your own for ye are bought with a price: therefore glorify God." Thus Christ "redeemed us" to God, out of every kindred blood and people and nation.

This is not all of the atonement and redemption but is one facet of this thrilling gem as we hold it up and flash the beams of God's word upon it. I want you to notice the characteristics of this Greek word, *agoradzo.* It means to "purchase in order to use." There is a utilitarian tone about it and it might be interesting for you to trace it.

You will find this word, *"ransomed," "redeemed," "purchased"* in Matthew 21:12, where it says that they purchased "doves" in the temple for sacrifice. In Mark 6:37, they "buy two hundred pennyworth of bread, and give them to eat." Bread is purchased, for one reason, in order that it may be used as edible food. In Matthew 13:44, a field is ransomed in order that the "treasure" that is buried within it might be secured. In Matthew 27:7, they purchase a burial plot to bury the dead. All such places are so to be used. In Revelation 3:18 they buy or purchase garments that they may "be clothed," and this is the only reason for the purchase of raiment. In I Corinthians 7:23, we are purchased as the "bondservants of Christ and not the servants of men." We are "purchased," "redeemed," to be used of Christ.

We may call this a possessive attribute of Calvary and of redemption. We are not our own, we are bought with the price, we are God's purchased ones. Peter admonishes us in his second epistle, the second chapter and the first verse, that "there shall be false teachers among you, who would insinuate destructive heresies, even denying the Lord that bought [or ransomed] them." To deny God's right of ownership over us would be a supreme mistake and a most tragic denial.

You and I might not debate intellectually the fact that we belong to God by purchase, but we might be guilty of this heresy if we do not live it out realistically and pragmatically. It is possible for Christ to "own" us and not to "possess" us. I own several umbrellas but I do not possess them—people borrowed them and have not returned them. You undoubtedly own some books that you do not possess; you have loaned them out and they have never been returned. They are "yours" but they are not at "your service." It is possible for us to be "His" and yet not be at "His service." It is quite possible that Christ *owns* us, because we were bought with the price, and yet does not *possess* us, because we are at the beck and call of other programs and other persons. We sometimes qualify this ownership in a half-hearted service and, realistically, we sometimes sing a famous hymn in this actual paraphrase:

"I'll go where you want me to go, dear Lord;
Real service is what I desire.
I'll sing a solo any time, Lord,
But don't ask me to sing in the choir.

"I'll say what you want me to say, dear Lord;
I want to see things come to pass;
But don't ask me to teach boys and girls, dear Lord;
I'd rather just stay in my class.

"I'll give what you want me to give, dear Lord;
I will that Thy kingdom should thrive.
I'll give you my nickels and dimes, dear Lord;
But please don't ask me to tithe.

"I'll do what you want me to do, dear Lord;
I'll say what you want me to say;
But I'm busy just now with myself, dear Lord;
I'll serve you some other day!"

To me there is a great hazard in some contemporary evangelism. Namely that we offer people *salvation* but do not call them to *service*. We emphasize the fact that in the redemption of Christ "they get out of something," but we do not also remind them that they "get in for something"—a life of service to God. Of course, we "get out of something"—there is a glorious gift of pardon for us all, and we do escape what otherwise would be the normal retribution and punishment for our transgressions.

But let us also remember that in this atonement we not only receive salvation, we are also purchased for service. We receive pardon for the sins of yesterday and, at the same time, we accept the program of His kingdom for tomorrow.

An Arab fed faithfully a beggar who was at his gate, but one day the Arab was in extreme difficulty and needed someone to run an errand for him immediately. He summoned the beggar and asked him to do the service, but the beggar drew himself up to his haughty height, and said, "I ask alms; I do not run errands!" How true that is of many of us. We ask alms of Christ—peace, pardon, power, His presence, and millions of other gifts; but we will not run His errands. We ask of Him, but we do not allow Him to ask of us. To us religion is more "intake" than it is "outgo." A great Chinese leader once said that one thing that surprised him in American laymen was that they were always talking about how much they could ask of God and so seldom of how much God was able to ask of them!

Yes, evangelism can become mere "escapism" if it is only a deliverance from something, but it must also be an "expedition" for Jesus Christ. Do not misunderstand me; I know that we are "saved by faith," but "*unto* good works" also, and salvation is to the end of service.

Did you ever stop to consider the various ways in

which men may be "lost"? There is the parable of the *lost sheep,* found in Luke 15. We may wander away and thus be lost in the labyrinth of our wondering, skeptical minds. We may at times go off to worship other gods and give ourselves to strange idols, and thus be "lost." The parable of the *prodigal son* in the same chapter reminds us that we can be lost by "wasting our living with harlots," by feeding on the husks of the world, by riotous living, by missing the purpose of life altogether. This need not even be argued.

There is also the parable of the *lost coin,* and may I remind you that nothing was the matter with the coin. I do not think it was counterfeit; it might not even have been soiled. It was probably one of the coins used to make up an engagement necklace. Until the woman found it she could not be married. So she searched diligently until she did find it. Only one thing was the matter—the coin was simply *lost,* it was simply *out of circulation,* it could not be found. You and I can be "lost" when we are merely out of circulation, when we are not where we should be, when God cannot find us, when we are merely "unavailable." Yes, this is as serious a sin as any of the others we have mentioned. Is the sin of unavailability to God as bad as the sin of adultery or of murder? Think it through! We can be as truly "lost" in the selfish pre-occupations of our lives as in any other way.

But someone might say, "Are we not saved because of the love of God?" "Herein God commendeth his love toward us in that while we were yet sinners Christ died for us." Quite true. Was it not said that He looked upon the young ruler and, looking upon him, "loved him"? Yes, but look at that word "love"—it is the Greek word *agapao*. It is not the love described by *phileo*, which means an unreasoning, emotional, gushing love. The word *agapao* means to love thinkingly and with reason; it means to "esteem" and to "prize" the thing you love. As Jesus looked at the young ruler, He "prized" him, He "esteemed" him, He wanted to use him; we might even say He "coveted" him.

A certain engineer was gazing at Niagara, watching its dynamic torrents plunging into the abyss in their determination to reach the sea. As he looked at the laughing eddies and all this potential power, he realized it was harnessed to nothing! Realizing the possibility of taking the power of a harnessed Niagara and applying its pressure to carbon atoms and thus making diamonds in seven days, which otherwise would have taken centuries to form, realizing all this tremendous potential of a harnessed Niagara, he lifted his eyes to the heavens and cried, "Oh, God, diamonds, diamonds!" Christ was looking at this young man with his unharnessed abilities and He loved him—He coveted him. Was He saying within His soul, "Oh, young man, if I could only change your foam into diamonds, and have you follow me!"

How often must Christ look upon the multitudes, even some who claim Him, and covet us for His service! A certain woman was looking at Niagara Falls, one of the seven wonders of the world, watching its dashing torrents and beauty. The guide said, "Well, madam, what do you think of that?" To which she replied, "Oh, isn't it cute?" That is all you can say of some women, "Aren't they cute?" Laughing, bubbling personalities, dashing, but harnessed to absolutely nothing. Useless in the Kingdom of God, with all of their potential power! One woman said, "Jesus Christ upsets me. It is said of Him that He 'went about doing good,' while I spend my time simply 'going about.'"

What wonderful things would happen in the church, what dynamic results, if this "possessive attribute of Calvary" would grip us all! How many words would be spoken day by day in the market place for things spiritual! How many men would walk out of darkness, learning for the first time to see because someone had led them into the light; how many tasks could be taken upon shoulders; how many classes could be taught; how many burdens could be lifted by men who realized that this was a part of their regal vow in service to God and to others!

Only two major forces are left in the world today, all others seem to be satellites. These are Communism

and Christianity. Their success or failure in this struggle will depend upon the ability of each movement to
commandeer the loyalty and service of its devotees.
Both Christians and Communists have the same strategy—the world for their cause. Both of them give
somewhat generously; both of them are sending their
men and women as agents to the far corners of the
earth with their particular message. But this question
remains: Will the passion of the "sign of the sickle" be
equalled by the passion of the "sign of the Cross"?
Will the possessive attribute of the Communists be
greater than the possessive attribute of ours? No king
or emperor ever was successful in conquest unless he
was able altogether to commandeer the service of his
people. And if Communism is able to secure more of
the persons, the program, the possessions, and the passions of its people than Christ is able to secure in this
day, it will go bad with the sign of the Cross.

Yet it might be said, "Is this not driving a rather
hard bargain? This 'life for a life,' this 'tit for tat,' this
saying to God, or God saying to us, 'You give me your
life and I will give you eternal life.' Does it not smack
of mere bargaining in the market place?" Scarcely that
—it is more generous than that! To think that the gift
of fifty-two years on the average of your life and mine
should bring us countless æons of years in an endless
life; that by one act, the surrender of ourselves, God
acts for us; that by going on this short-lived expedition

for Him, He should proffer us eternity; that by giving God myself, God gives me Himself! Why, it is not even reasonable; it would be utterly ridiculous were it not born of the tremendous love of God.

But this is not *slavery*—this *fellowship* with Christ. If it is, it is a bondage of golden chains that never chafe. You remember that Jesus said to His disciples, "I call you not *servants,* but I call you *friends."* It is Christ who is willing to lift us up until we stand with Him, walk with Him, talk with Him, fellowship with Him. This is the most thrilling experience possible to human life.

But may I remind you that we came to this friendship through the obedience of servants? "Ye are my friends if ye do whatsoever I command you." Only as we *obey* Him can we step into this friendship.

Once we have done that, there is something exalted about this position. He who "took upon himself the form of a servant" as our King. And thus wishing to serve, we, too, become kings, as suggested in our text. When we enjoy this daily royal walk with Him we shall exclaim at the end of this life, "The half has not been told!"

And they brought young children to him, that he should touch them. . . . And he took them up in his arms, put his hands upon them, and blessed them. . . . And he was gone forth into the way.

MARK *10:13, 16, 17*

The King's Secret

YES, THEN CHRIST WAS ON HIS WAY—ANY KING OR leader who knows the importance of youth is "on his way" to empire and to power!

America is doomed to capture in spite of all of her defenses of Army, Navy, Marines and Air! Before long, an army will march across the stretches of our great land; its soldiers will march into the White House and place there their own Chief Magistrate and elect their own Congress. They will commandeer our ample rivers, our commodious harbors and our matchless resources. They will take over our mint and all its wealth. They will go into our churches and preach what they will, into our schools and teach what they will. Nothing you and I can do will ever protect us against this marching army—we are doomed to capture! That army is in training now. You can hear the tramp of their marching feet. It is the army of youth!

I want to talk to you today about the strategy of

youth. Do not turn off the radio because you might
not happen to be a parent. We all are affecting this
kingdom, because every one of us affects youth somewhere, some time, some place. Remember on the golf
course when you sliced the ball badly and it was lost
in the rough? The caddy had done his best to find it
and finally you said, "Never mind, son, that was a hard
one to find. We have another one." Or did you swear
and give him a good going over? You touched a kingdom that day! You said something to a youth's fertile
mind and it gave birth to a doubt or to a great faith.
You touched an empire! He overheard you telling a
story one day; it had a splendid lift to it. That was ex-
cellent! Or was it off color and did it leave a question-
able deposit in his mind forever? You touched a
kingdom that day! You paid your taxes; that was not
easy, but out of a part of those well-earned dollars a
school was fashioned by the state and a mind was
shaped in turn. You touched an empire when you
wrote that check! You sang a lullaby one night and
quieted a frightened little soul or he went to sleep the
other day after a marital argument at the table—his
little heart, like a sensitive seismograph, registering
every domestic earthquake and quarrel. You touched
a kingdom that day!

He sold you a newspaper on the corner; you were
irritable because he was slow in poking the change
through the car window or you said, smilingly, "Keep

the change, son." You touched an empire that day! In that table conversation, in that bigoted tirade against someone of another race, you did your work or, with a great sweep of conversation that took in people of all races with the tenderness of your concern, you set his heart on a broad road of love. You touched a kingdom that day! Yes, every day we shape a child, thinkingly or unthinkingly, as mothers, fathers, grandparents, brothers, sisters, friends, teachers, merchants, sportsmen. We all touch clay and when it sets forever into the hardness of maturity, we all will have helped to shape some kind of a kingdom.

There is little need in asking the question, "What will youth do with us tomorrow?" Because the question is answered in one we must ask of ourselves, "What are we doing with them today?" Youth is simply clay in the hands of the potter. There is factually and actually no youth problem, it is always an adult problem. We make them what they are. If we do not like the dresses they wear, we cut them; if we do not like the books they read, we write them; if we do not like the films they see, as adults we make them; if we do not like what they believe, some of us believed it before them; if we do not like what they do, let us remember that they are but imitators of someone else of greater maturity. Yet that child comes to us with destiny within him, and tomorrow will be the echo of what he is today.

47

I am the Child.
All the world waits for my coming.
All the earth watches with interest to see what I shall
  become.
Civilization hangs in the balance,
For what I am, the world of tomorrow will be.

I am the Child.
I have come into your world, about which I know nothing.
Why I came I know not;
How I came I know not.
I am curious; I am interested.

I am the Child.
You hold in your hand my destiny.
You determine, largely, whether I shall succeed or fail.
Give me, I pray you, those things that make for happiness.
Train me, I beg you, that I may be a blessing to the world.*

All strong leaders have recognized this. Goethe
said that the future of any nation, at any given moment, lay in the opinions of its youth under twenty-five
years of age. Christ put a child in the midst and said,
"Of such is the kingdom of God." Hitler must first
commandeer his Hitler Youth before he is on his way,
and Mussolini must call the youths of Italy and place
them in the "Giovanne Italienne," composed of millions of young girls in their teens, and he must organize
his Italian boys in the "Balilla" while they march in

*"The Child's Appeal," by Mamie Gene Cole, from *Mas-
terpieces of Religious Verse*. (Harper and Brothers, 1948. By
permission).

48

their black shirts in the shadows of the Piedmont. Then Mussolini is "on his way." Dr. Paul Payne said some time ago, "If you want to change the whole civilization overnight—start with the children. If you want to plant a conviction indelibly in society, plant it in the hearts of children." As the twig is bent, so grows the tree.

Jesus Christ, realizing this secret of kingdom strategy, warned us constantly lest we "offend one of these little ones."

Out of what might these offenses arise?

First of all, we may certainly offend youth by holding from them the right sort of *spiritual instruction* in a day like this. When the body of the child fails to grows physically and at the age of fifty he still has the stature of a child of five, it is distressing. When, mentally, at the age of forty a person still has the intellect of a child of four, it leads us to tragedy and tears. But when a child grows up to the age of fifty and maintains the spiritual stature of a child of five, that, above all, is most distressing and pathetic!

A woman came into my office one day, tears coursing down her cheeks, and said, "Dr. Evans, there is no God in our home, no prayer, no thanks, no grace at the table. I cannot tell you what it means, to wake up and realize that you have married only a spiritual adolescent!" How pathetic that arrestment of growth is! We must start early. It is estimated that twenty-seven mil-

49

lion boys and girls of a certain age bracket in America are without any systematic religious instruction—as pagan as though they had been born in the South Seas or in the African jungle. It has been said that only eight per cent of the youth of New York City have any connection with the church between the ages of sixteen and twenty-five. One per cent attend Jewish services, less than two per cent attend Protestant church services, and less than five per cent attend Catholic services; ninety-two per cent are not reached by any religious group! What a spiritual offense!

We need dynamic spiritual *leadership* for youth today. It was said that Hitler in his youth movement was able to secure one man to train every eight boys. The same thing was true of Mussolini. These men were not too busy to teach a sense of empire to their youth and, along the Italian hills, one man marched with every eight boys, teaching them, in their enthusiasm for the Roman empire, to sing, "Italia, Italia, Beloved!" That was power!

One of the most difficult tasks in training youth today is also to find women who will punctuate their busy or cluttered-up lives sufficiently to give leadership to the young girlhood of the present day. What do you think would happen in America if, for every girls' club and every Sunday-school class of eight, we could find one woman to give faithfully of her leadership? The womanhood of today spends a lot of time in the art

50

clubs painting pictures but too little time splashing upon the canvas of young lives a high motif and beauty of character. There are more women interested in garden clubs, the nurture of gladioli and onions, than in growing the fine flower of youth in the gardens of their communities. There are many men at the golf course more interested in sinking a little white ball into a little round hole in par than in teaching a boy where the goal of life is and to play the game of life in a commendable score. A lot of youths are going down in this game of life simply for the lack of someone to coach them.

Aristotle once said, "Those who train children are worthy of double the honor of those who merely bear them." It is not always difficult to *bear* children—it is more difficult to *train* them!

Let us be void of all offense to youth in our *own homes*. It is true that the hand that rocks the cradle rules the world but we are living in a day in which there are many parents who have washed their hands of the spiritual obligations toward their children while their lives are filled with a thousand-and-one multiform activities. They farm out their children to other leaderships, particularly in the realm of the spirit. In a certain home the mother had died; the family altar and family worship had gone into the discard and, finally, one Sunday morning about church time a lad crawled up into his father's lap and leaning against the smoking jacket in which his father was lounging said, "Daddy dear, is God dead?" He is actually in many a home today. One father said, "When it comes to being a priest to my boy at home, I either 'skid or skiddoo.' "

We forget that "every time a boy goes wrong, a good man dies"—and there are too many casualties of this type in the United States of America. Too many fathers are *sending* their children to Sunday school instead of *taking* them. It is said by some psychologists that we learn eight times as much through the sense of sight as through any of the other senses. What children see us do speaks more loudly than what we tell them to do. "Age needs critics but youth needs models." No amount of precept which we proffer our children will ever take the place of the practice of our lives.

Fathers, in the sphere of your kingly parental influence, it will not be enough for you to offer your son a check. You must proffer him Christian character for his example. It will not be enough for you faithfully to feed his body, you must also protect his young soul from malnutrition. It will not be enough, mother, in choosing the right school for your daughter, to be sure that there she learns merely to hold a fork properly, take part in clever conversation—she must have something worth saying. It will not be enough to teach her to ride a horse or to walk up the steps with grace; she must know where she is going!

God grant that when your children come of age,

when they are so tall that physically they may look down on you because of their height, they may always be able to look up to you because of the height of your soul! This was expressed in a poem by Dorothy Markham Brown, entitled "A Growing-up Son."

It seems but such a little while
    Since he was playing at my knee,
And when I spoke to him, my eyes
    Would downward turn his face to see.
And now, in just a few short years,
    (O God, how short the years can be!)
My eyes must upward turn, for then
    He will be looking down on me.

Dear God, if in the years gone by
    I have been in some measure fit
To merit childhood's upturned gaze,
    And only quail a little bit,
Please help me in the coming years
    A nobler woman yet to be—
That when his eyes must downward turn,
    His soul will still look up to me." *

God will simply have to give this world a new sheet to write on in this new generation, otherwise the paper of this social order will fold in the same old creases—war, chaos, materialism, and distrust. "If any man be in Christ, he is a new creature: old things are passed away." We must start with inside regeneration

* *Good Housekeeping Magazine*, 1944.

and the individual must become "new." Then he will be able to move up and change things about him—the whole collective society.

There is no guarantee as to what youth will do with this world tomorrow, save as it lies in what you and I are doing with youth today. It will be wholly theirs and this is the time to speak, and what they say with tomorrow's dawning will, of course, be what you and I have said in today's sunset.

54

If any man be in Christ, he is a new creature.

II CORINTHIANS *5:17*

These Are the King's People

Two gigantic tasks face christ as a king. One is a future task—that of preparing a kingdom. He said, "I go to prepare a place for you. In my Father's house are many mansions." He will not have much difficulty in fashioning these dwelling places. But the second and more difficult task is that of preparing the souls of men to dwell in these mansions. A certain clergyman was showing some beautiful residences in one of the elite districts of the town to a visiting friend of his. The guest declared, "These are certainly palatial homes." To which the clergyman replied, "It is not so difficult to build mansions as it is to grow princely men to dwell in them!" That will always be a task. It is far easier for a city to fashion houses than it is to fashion human hearts, to produce palaces than princely people, to erect mansions than to build men who are a credit to the city.

If Christ is a king—and He is—then that kingship

will be empty unless He has fit subjects over whom to rule. The strength and reputation of any king lies in his people, his ability to govern them, use them, command them, and shape them. King George was quite at the mercy of the conduct of the Britishers; Queen Wilhelmina will naturally be judged by her Hollanders; Christ will naturally be judged by His followers.

Historically, Jesus will rule in principality and power; we are confident that the last maps will always be made in heaven! But this rule is not always inevitable over your little life and destiny and mine. There are times when God will be able to determine the course of the history of nations with more ease than He can determine the course of the little empire of your heart and mine, since He has endowed us with free will. Indeed, He is as interested in the human soul as He is in the movement of nations.

One soul, one life, means more to God than certain courses of history. By first saying Himself, "What shall it profit a man if he gain the whole world and lose his own soul?" He has permitted us to say,

> Were the whole realms of nature mine
> That were a present far too small;
> Love so amazing, so divine,
> Demands my soul, my life, my all.*

* Presbyterian Hymnal, "When I Survey The Wondrous Cross," by Isaac Watts.

Therefore, somewhere within the whole spiritual economy of His empire there must be the power to create and mold a kingly people.

This becomes possible by Christian conversion. When we receive Christ, we receive the life of Christ, we are engrafted into His body, and the sap of His vital self becomes a part of that inner nourishment that causes us to bear the Christian fruits of the spirit. Without this the characteristics which we possess will be superficial and not native to us. The baubles and decorations of the Christmas tree are not native to it and, consequently, when you jostle the tree they fall to the floor in pathetic breakage. But apples do not need to be artificially fastened to an apple tree. They are native to it and grow normally on its branches. Your Christian graces and mine will be superficial, purely ornamental and pretended, unless Christ indwells us. When He does, we shall be normally kind, normally forgiving, normally moral and normally courageous. By our fruits shall they know us.

The acceptance of the cross of Christ and His redemption is something more than merely a *forgiveness*. It is also the *force* which enables us to live a life. The redemption of God is something more than the erasing rubber at the end of a pencil. It is also the lead by which we write a Christian life on the sheet of our days.

The transfusion of the life of Christ into our veins

59

enables Him to become a part of us and us of Him.

This is a very unique relationship. "If any man be *in Christ,* he is a new creature." You notice how intimate that is. We are *in Christ* and Christ is *in us.* That is not merely saying "hello" to him, that is not merely saluting Him; but Christ is *in us* and has become *a part* of us. Paul said, "It is not I that liveth, but Christ that liveth *in me"*—not *"with me."*

In baptism we are "baptized into one body" and become a part of that body, Jesus Christ being its Head. This is the glory of the Church; it is in this sense quite unique and apart from any other organization in the world. When you elect the President of the United States you do not become a part of the President, nor does the President become part of you. When you join a club you do not become a part of its president; when you matriculate in a school, within you is not the blood and life of the president of the university or of your professor; when you enlist in an army you are not one with the commander, nor is he a part of you; but when we rightly come into the Church we come into the Body of Christ. We are suddenly "organs one of another," "we are members of his body, of his flesh and of his bones." Christ not only lives *with* us, He lives *in* us. The Church is the only organization in the world in which its true members partake of the life of their Founder and their King.

In the days of Christ, as He was choosing the first

men for His Church, He selected men of passions and faults like yours and mine; but He evidenced the power to change them! He found Matthew—mercenary, commercial, selling his birthright for cash and commission, metallic, his god more a Roman coin than God. Yet Christ changed him, and, forsaking all, Matthew marched after the souls of men. Now, James, selfish, introverted, hedonistic, wanting the right hand at the throne of Christ, finally finds that the glory of life lies in works of goodness, kindness, and unselfishness. Christ finds John, a man irascible and of bad disposition, "Boanerges—a son of thunder," but when Christ is done with him he becomes the great apostle of love and self-effacement. He finds Thomas, ever stumbling over his mind, intellectually slow to believe; but he finally cries, "My Lord and my God" and marches to a great kingliness of faith. He calls Simon Peter, impulsive, bragging, making great boasts but bogging down in the face of the mores of the crowd; but finally Peter is willing to be crucified head downward for his Lord. Out of Mary he will cast seven devils—whatever they were—and will give to us one of the most beautiful characters of history.

This is one of the outstanding characteristics of His early kingdom, His ability to change ordinary people into kingly persons.

There must be no limit to this sort of power, even across the great cosmic area. He will take the Druids and their brutal sacrifices and change them into the Welshmen with their marching hymns of the love of God. He will take the cursing, ravaging Huns and later give us Luther and Niemoeller and the Reformation. He will take the Japanese mind, bloody and cruel and narrow, and with the aid of His gospel, proclaimed since the last war under able leadership, and give us a group of people who are to be trusted even in this turmoil. He will take the Anglo-Saxons, "rough and tough," guilty of human sacrifices and barbaric, and through Augustine bring to them a kingly gospel, and the following centuries will find them civilized and in their right minds, native barbarians plus the power of Christ to change. He will go into the South Sea islands in the person of a missionary who discovers the hands of other missionaries eaten at a feast just before he arrived, and, later on, as a result of this imperial changing power, "fuzzy-wuzzies" that once were cannibals will be carrying a soldier tenderly to the dressing station, described in the words of an Australian who enjoyed this experience on a stretcher:

Though they haven't any haloes, only holes slashed
    through the ear,
Their faces marked with tattoos, and scratch pins in their
    hair,
Bringing back the deadly wounded, just as steady as a
    hearse
Using leaves to keep the rain off, and as gentle as a nurse,

May the mothers in Australia, when they offer up a prayer,
Mention these impromptu angels with the fuzzy-wuzzy
   hair.*

You and I as the King's people must take care that
this imperial power of Christ to change does not seem
to break down with too many exceptions in our personal lives. Of course, no king's son or daughter ever
at every moment wholly lived up to this holy seal and
high escutcheon. There are moments in our lives
when we all have forgotten this nobility and this heri-
tage, for we all have sinned and come short of the glory
of God; but with Him there is plenteous redemption
and forgiveness.

But let us remember that with this pardon must
always come a power over sin. Without His forgiveness, we have the power but we keep our guilt. On the
other hand, if we receive His pardon of our sins and do
not also receive His power over our sins, then we have
lost our guilt but keep the weakness. It is this kingly
balance in our lives, then, that we must always crave—
His pardon for the sins of yesterday and His growing
power over the sins of tomorrow.

We are very much afraid today of being over-
souled. The hypocrisy of yesterday lay in the fact
that people pretended to be better than they were.
The hypocrisy of today lies in the fact that many

* "The Fuzzy-Wuzzy Angels of the Kokoda Trail," by
Sapper Beros.

people pretend to be worse than they really are. There seems to be an inherent embarrassment about acting royally, but when you and I are actually in this kingdom we are not afraid of being over-souled. Our kingly behavior should be normal with us. The eagle is not afraid that when he flies in the sky he will have too much light. Imagine a fish crying, "Cast me not into the water, lest I drown." Imagine a sunflower refusing to turn toward the sun lest it receive too much of its lifegiving rays. You and I have never lived— truly lived—until our lives are lost with God in Christ.

The one thing that gave Paul's message power was the fact that for the first time in history a religious *philosophy* carried with it a life changing *force*. When he gave his deliverance on Mars Hill, he seemed to fail utterly before the stuffy minds of Greeks gathered there on the hill; but the Christian slaves later came to save his gospel because while they could not *outargue* the Greeks, they could *outlive* their Grecian masters, and the Christian ladies-in-waiting lived better lives than the pagan women who had hired them. Yes, there was a religious *philosophy* that carried with it a life-changing *force*, and then they trailed after Christ, the great philosophers of Greece, Chrysostum, Athanasius, the two Gregories, Justin Martyr, and Origen the keenest of them all, declaring that the "highest philosophy was fulfilled in Jesus Christ." Here was something, at long last, that "worked," and the Christian will always be the greatest argument for Christianity.

Two young men had heard a certain skeptic give his address in a public hall, and, coming out, one of the collegians said to the other, "Well, I guess he knocked the props out from under Christianity that time, didn't he?" "Oh, no," said the other collegian, "he has not explained my mother's life, and until he explains my mother's life I will stay by my mother's God." The greatest apologetics for Christianity lie in the Christian life. There is little to be said against the King when His subjects live royally.

This is a practical and experimental age. The average college man would botanize on his mother's grave; he demands proof and demonstration. In such a pragmatic age, our believing will have to produce living. History wants to look at the facts; psychology wishes to see the effect of believing on action; religious philosophy demands a corroborating experience. "Good preaching will yield the reasonableness of Christianity, but good living will evidence its power!" In this sense the Kingdom of Christ is at the mercy of the King's people.

Some black African slaves were marching in chains toward the ship that would take them to the land of slavery. They were shuffling along, discouraged, melancholy. with heads bowed toward the ground. But one young man walked with a kingly bearing, with head thrown back and shoulders squared. One of the

slave drivers asked, "Who is that man?" To this another slave driver replied, "He is the son of an African
king, and he cannot forget it!" While other men are
shuffling along, discouraged, uncouth, unprincely, may
you and I say within our souls, "I am a child of the
King, and I cannot forget it." Such will be the glory
of His empire.

Peace I leave with you, my peace I give unto you: not as the world giveth, give I unto you. Let not your heart be troubled, neither let it be afraid.

JOHN 14:27

America and the King

THE CRY COMES UP FROM WRECKED CITIES, BOMBED hamlets, the frozen wastes of Korea; from American homes unbombed but restless with foreboding of the star shells of dreams of what is happening to our sons, of the possibilities of atomic explosions, the pressures of military treasuries, vacant chairs, widows, broken homes, and an uncertain tomorrow. Why can we not have peace? We can—God wants it—it is up to us. But above that cry, "God, we would have peace," comes the call of truth, "But you must pay for it, work for it."

There is a great deal of argument about armaments. This is not the occasion for that—at least I shall not make it so. We all wish that these enormous armaments could be done away with. But before we can disarm ourselves with safety—for never again must we have too little and too late—we must take to ourselves a great spiritual rearmament.

Before we could scrap our present navies with

safety we should have to float a new spiritual navy to take its place. In that great flotilla and fleet of the spirit must be included these ships: Worship, Stewardship, Kinship, and Leadership.

We must come back to the *worship of God* in Christ. Men become like the beings they worship. They take on the color and tone of their gods, real or imagined. America started out with God. We are spiritually a monarchy in one sense. Our history and our hopes are well written in these lines of the hymn we love:

Our fathers' God, to Thee, Author of liberty, to Thee we
    sing:
Long may our land be bright with freedom's holy light;
Protect us by Thy might, great God, our King.

He has always been our King—this has been a nation in which all men wished to be royal but in which no man cared to wear a crown. That was for God to do. We began a nation that wished to worship Christ.

When our Pilgrim fathers gathered before the light of the smoking lamp aboard the *Mayflower,* before they landed at Plymouth, they penned these lines of the Mayflower Compact: "We whose names are underwritten . . . have undertaken for the glory of God to establish in the northern parts of Virginia the first colony for the advancement of the Christian faith." Coming here for the express purpose of worshiping

70

God according to the dictates of their own conscience, they came here to establish a nation in which it would be demonstrated what would happen to any people who cared and dared to follow Jesus Christ.

Our democracy was born and has been sustained in Christian principles. Our type of democracy will not "democ" well without Christ. "In the beauty of the lilies Christ was born across the sea, with a glory in His bosom that transfigures you and me," and when Christ was brought to these shores our glory began.

Worship is a reaching up for the aid of God and a happy, hearty obedience to His will and way. May we never forget that. The trouble is that our efforts for armistice and peace have been largely on the horizontal humanistic level. We need the upward tug of the Spirit that comes from sincere worship and work.

If you were to take ten balls, place them on a table and strive with the horizontal force of a cue stick to herd them together by force and blow into a compact group, you would probably succeed only in scattering them. But affix to each single ball, with some Scotch tape, a single piece of string, then take these several string ends in your hand and exert an upward pull— what will happen? These scattered balls will by every law of physics nestle together in a close knit of fraternity of spheres.

We have tried faithfully and pathetically to drive nations and peoples together by horizontal force—by wars, regimentations, treaties, pressures, and police force, and we have but scattered them, and hearts today are bruised and brittle and far from a concourse of nations.

If we could but affix to each nation the upward pull of the love of God, if we would but permit Christ to take in His royal hands these threads of the nations' hearts and exert that upward tug, we would see the peoples and the nations nestling together in the brotherhood and security of the spheres that we so earnestly desire. But this will be of the Spirit.

We need to launch the ship of a new spiritual *Stewardship*. How we spend our money! Two things you and I can do with it—we can plant it or bury it. We "bury" it when we spend it on things that yield no spiritual or lasting harvest. We "plant" it when we spend it and invest it in things that spiritually abide. In one year we shall spend nearly fifty billion dollars in arming our hands with weapons of defense and offense. At the same time Americans will spend approximately two billion dollars on religion—on arming our hearts with God and for great goals—one twenty-fifth as much!

Great generals are saying today that the "military has had its last chance." There are only certain things the military can do. They can open the doors of nations so that truth may march in—the dictators and enslavers of men's souls having been pushed aside by force.

The military can deliver the "anæsthetic" only It can "knock out" Japan and Germany and strap them to the table. Then it must invite the doctors of the spirit—the religious leaders, that they with the instruments of the spirit may operate and remove bad ideologies, wrong theologies, and cancerous feelings. If we fail to do that, then, when the conquered nation, the patient, comes out of the anæsthetic in an armistice, he will be the same as before he was put under by force.

MacArthur pleaded for 3000 missionaries for Japan. We sent him 124. The military anæsthetic was thorough, but where were the doctors? Well, the handful of missionaries in Japan did a wonderful task, and today Japan is the most hopeful of all the occupied lands. Why? Because after we had delivered the anæsthetic of war we took our instruments of the Spirit, for, as one general said, "It was a theological war," and having operated on the theology of Japan, she arose a new nation. After the Marines had given them a "licking," the missionaries gave them a "light."

At home one government official stated that the $40,000 a certain Board of National Missions of a certain denomination had spent on evangelizing the American Indian had saved the people of America and the government in taxes $4,000,000 in that same period of time that otherwise would have had to be spent on

73

putting down Indian rebellions. The love of Christ and a sensible Christian stewardship had given back to us $100 for every $1 we had given to God.

When will we as Americans wake up to this wise stewardship? A great leader said before the Pacific War, "If we don't send ten times as many missionaries to Japan in the next ten years to change her theology, we shall send 100,000 Marines." We did not send the missionaries, so we had to send the Marines. It cost us $40,000 a year per Marine, and perhaps his dear life; it would have cost us $4,000 a year per missionary. What bad bankers we are! From the bridge of this Ship of Stewardship I hear this challenging cry:

"Give of Thy sons to bear this message glorious;
Give of Thy wealth to speed them on their way:
Pour out thy soul for them in prayer victorious
And all thou spendest Jesus will repay."

We need a new sense of *Kinship,* a new concept of the unity of the races of Christ. "God has made of one blood all the nations of the earth." Do we honestly believe that?

The world has been torn in tragic blood conceits. When the black men of Ethiopia ran the then known world of the 25th Dynasty, thinking themselves to be the superpeople, they started a war. When the Greeks under arrogant Alexander thought they were the superpeople, they brought about the Grecian wars. When

74

Cæsar said, *Civis Romanus sum*—"a citizen of Rome am I"—and when only those of Roman blood were honored; when the Roman eagle wished to flap his massive wings over all peoples, all that started the Roman wars. When Napoleon, drunk with French pride, commanded every soldier to carry about in his knapsack a map of the world in the tricolors of France, he arrogantly precipitated the Napoleonic wars. When the Kaiser cried *Deutschland über alles*—"Germany over everyone"—that incubated the First World War. When Hitler swaggered and spoke of the Germans as being the "supermen" destined to rule the world, that started the first half of the Second World War, and Hirohito, pretending to be the 125th descendant of the sun goddess Amaterasu, and so destined to rule the world, started the other half of that world war.

Let us guard against our own Anglo-Saxon conceits of blood. There are plenty of Anglo-Saxons today who think they should rule the world. These race prejudices—this sinking of the good Ship Kinship, this scuttling of the Cruiser Brotherhood—could mean our destruction. God deliver us from arrogant racial conceits.

I have nothing against a family tree, but the best thing to do with it is to spray it! Keep from it the bugs and scales of pride, conceit, and arrogance. Let us remember that the taller our concept of God, the broader our concept of brotherhood. "By this shall all men know that ye are my disciples, if ye love one another." The moment God is my Father, He also becomes the Father of another man, and that man becomes my brother. We dare not reach out and accept the privileges of the Fatherhood of God without also accepting the responsibilities of the Brotherhood of Man.

Then let us launch the *Ship of Leadership*. America should lead the way. We have had the kiss of God since our earliest national birth. We have had the light. America, if she is to maintain her place of leadership, must get back to God and morals. When the doctor sees that a superficial scab has grown over a wound but that the infection still lies beneath the scab —he pulls off the scab, and the wound bleeds again. Any wound must heal from the "inside out." We have won another war, and across the wound of this world has grown a superficial scab of military victory; but beneath there still is selfishness, sin, jealousy, godlessness. So the Great Physician pulls the scab off, and we bleed again.

So shall it ever be until we are willing to cry out, "Create in me a clean heart, O God, and renew a right spirit within me."

I said to the fine men at West Point Military Academy some time ago, "Gentlemen, we can never expect God to give us a lasting victory over our enemies until first we have won a spiritual victory over ourselves!"

76

Let us close by making this personal. Let us not dodge our personal responsibilities for peace this day by blaming President Truman or even by going back to Herbert Hoover, as some still do. The trouble is with us—John Does—citizens. US spells "us." There the trouble lies.

Living at peace with our next-door neighbor will help this problem, parent. Your child, too, can make his simple contribution to peace as in the words of Minnie Case Hopkins:

I tucked him in, then stooped beside his bed
To hear him say his prayers. "God bless us all," he said,
"An' please help me be good so I won't fight
That ol' McKelvie boy no more. Amen. Good night."
Good night, my little son. Thanks for your prayer for
    peace.
God help us to be good; then wars will quickly cease.*

We have not taken out of our own hearts the combustibles of war. If we cannot live at peace with each other in our own little homes, how can we expect nations to live at peace with each other around this great cosmic hearthside?

* *Good Housekeeping Magazine.*

*Seek ye first the kingdom of God, and his righteous-
ness.*

MATTHEW *6:33*

The Regal Home

No great kingdom is a success or long endures unless it can build durable homes.

God has set men together in governable portions. *Nations* as a whole are hard to handle—they are so huge, expansive, and collective. At the other extreme, *individuals,* too, are difficult to manage and to govern. The hope lies in the middle ground, at least in part, in the *family.* The story of civilization would, to a great degree, be the story of hearthsides.

Individuals are often at the mercy of the home. Marriage does as much as anything to make a man's life a sigh or a song. It certainly colors a woman's life. It often makes or breaks the human spirit. Psychologists have told us that very seldom do they see a case of disintegration of personality in a child but that it comes from either an unhappy or a broken home. Yes, as individuals we are highly colored by the nature of the domicile in which we dwell.

The same is true of nations. They, too, are at the

mercy of the hearthside. Napoleon once said that the future of France lay in its homes. That was true. A great Roman historian claimed that Rome began to fall when its homes began to disintegrate. We know that in France there were very few divorces until the bars were let down for the disintegration of the home. Then the French Revolution struck and France nearly died. In America there was a day when we had but one divorce in about five hundred marriages; it crept up to one divorce in every one hundred, then one divorce in every twelve, now there is one divorce in nearly every three or four, and it is prophesied that in five years we shall have one divorce for every 1.52 marriages. No nation is stronger than its homes, and when the homes decay the nation is on its way to decay. This, of course, is also true of the spiritual Kingdom of God. The heart of the church lies in its hearthsides.

The home, first of all, is God's *theological seminary*. It is here that He most fittingly and powerfully explains Himself. He takes the relationships of the home and makes them the tutors and teachers of His own character and personality. "Like as a Father pitieth his children . . ." and we understand the pity of God in a father's love, his easy forgiveness of our mischief, his constant daily provision and the fact that his heart is like a barometer indicating all the storms that touch our lives. "As one whom his mother comforteth, so will I comfort you . . ." and through a mother's compassion and understanding we better see and understand the illimitable love of God. Christ "sticketh closer than a brother," and it is true that through the unselfish, fraternal love of the household we understand the unquenchable love of Christ. "Husbands love your wives, even as Christ also loved the church and gave himself for it." We should be able, through the experience of marriage, to come to an appreciation of the high relationship that Christ sustains to His Church. To some this relationship thus becomes beautiful; to others it has become a chamber of horrors. You see that by domestic symbolisms God wishes to explain Himself. Therefore, when you destroy a home you destroy a theological seminary, a university in which the soul goes to school to God.

If you want to strike at a spiritual kingdom, strike at its homes. It is perfectly evident that if religion does not work in the small area of thirty feet by thirty feet—the average American home—you cannot expect it to work in the town; if it does not work in the town, it will not work in the state; if it does not work in the state, it will not work in the nation; if it does not work in the nation, how could we expect it to work throughout the world? One loving, colored mammy once said, "If religion don't work at home, it's no good no place!" Who knows that better than a maid? One of the greatest things said of the Early Christian Church was, "What women these men have in their homes."

We are all mindful of the fact that it is most difficult to build homes today to withstand the social pressures of the hour. In the olden days we used to build our cathedrals and support them by flying buttresses, stones piled up and arched high. They were held together by *outside pressure*. Today more often are they built with inner ties—cantilever construction hidden in the masonry. The home of yesterday was held together by social pressures. A divorced person was scorned and socially isolated; a home could not afford to be broken. Now the situation is quite reversed and the pressures of society are likely to crash our homes on our heads. There is nothing in society to keep our homes together. They will more likely disintegrate under these social exactions, worries, and pressures if we are not careful; the home that survives today has inner ties—cantilever construction of character within its soul.

One of the great assets of a home today is a royal *purpose* at its center. "Seek ye first the kingdom of God, and his righteousness." "For me to live is Christ." Build the solar universe of your home around that sun and it is likely to be held together through stress and strain.

I was talking with a man who was being released from the armed forces after the recent war. He wore a pair of silver wings. He said to me, "Dr. Evans, I am engaged to be married. I am in love." To which I re-

plied, "You needn't tell me that. You have been glow-
ing like a Bunsen burner on this train for two days!"
"But I have a problem," he said. I replied, "Most
lovers do. What is yours?" He explained, "I am engaged to marry the daughter of one of the wealthiest
bankers in our town. If I do what she wants me to,
namely go into business with her father, I will receive
three times the salary I would if I do what I want to
do." "What do you want to do?" I asked. He answered, "I want to be a teacher at my alma mater and
shape the lives of men. But what I want to know is
this: would she be happy on one-third rations?" "Of
course, I do not know her, so I cannot answer your
question," I replied, "but, by the way, what is she living for? That would decide it." He said, in some
wonderment, "Well, I don't think I know. We never
discussed that." "By the way, what are you living for?"
I asked. To which he replied, "You've got me there,
sir." Then I said to him, "You know the thing that
keeps the solar system together is the fact that a great
sun is at the center and these planets are held to it.
Put anything less than the sun at the center and the
whole system would fly to pieces. The thing that will
keep your home together in the future is having at its
center a great central 'sun,' a great spiritual aim and
purpose. Without that, your home may fly to pieces
as others have done." Then I asked, "Why are you being married?" "Well," he said glowingly, "you see, I

love her and she loves me." "Well, if that is all," I replied, "then you would get very tired of that after a while. You see, you are trying to put her at the center of your universe and say, 'You are my sunshine, my golden sunshine.' But she will have weaknesses and you will discover that you cannot make a god out of your wife, nor she a god out of you. When you marry you should unite on something, someone taller than yourselves." He said, "Dr. Evans, we have nothing, but we are going to talk that over and I promise you we will have a central sun in our home." "Make it the Son of God," I added, "and you will find that He is a great adhesive and that nothing will pull you to pieces."

You see, the American home, any home, is an equilateral triangle. Husband and wife make two sides and God is the base that will hold it together. While there is a divorce in one out of every three or four American homes, someone has said that there is only one divorce out of every fifty-seven church homes. Why? There is something in the centrality of Christ that will give you fifteen to twenty times the chance of holding your home together if He becomes the base on which it is built.

We also need religion in the home in presenting to our children a reasonable religious authority. What every compass needs is a magnetic north; without it the needle of the compass vacillates crazily and without direction, and every home must establish for itself a moral ultimate, a magnetic north which says, "This is the way."

This so-called rebellion of youth against authority is not always a rebellion against "Authority," it is a rebellion against "no authority." Many parents are religiously unsure of what they think and what they believe, and their children know it and, naturally, do not look to their parents as the final court of appeal. There is no family altar, and, consequently, a home is deprived of that great seat of all authority—"thus said the Lord." The moment a parental idea has no other ground for authority than the fact that a parent happens to believe it, if it has no basis in the commands of God or the concepts of God, then that moment the child is under no particular obligation to believe the parental mind as against that of a friend, the gang, the teacher, or the town. Every home must have above it a fixed point—God.

The home is also sustained by the Godly relationship between husband and wife: "Whom therefore God hath joined together, let no man put asunder," and when God joins two people together they are likely to stay together. You see, husband and wife are like the spokes in a wheel, the closer they get to the same hub, the closer, naturally, they get to each other.

Paul and Mary were having a very hard time in their college courtship, and everyone prophesied that their marriage would go on the rocks. But five years of marriage have passed and they are living very happily together. Paul gave this as his secret of their success and tranquility: "We began our married life by prayer —audible prayer. That first evening together we knelt at the bedside and I asked God audibly to make me a thoughtful husband and to bless my Mary. Mary, timidly at first, for she was not used to audible prayer, asked God to make her a thoughtful wife and to bless me, her husband. We have found through the years that when two people are near to God it is very difficult for them to get away from each other."

Can you give me the name and address of any couple who went to the divorce court who prayed together to God on their knees—I said *together*—a week before they went? Christ is a great adhesive. It is a physical law that two objects close to the same thing must be close to each other, and it is a spiritual law that two persons close to God will normally be close to each other.

The home must be a regal place if Christ is King! If He is there, there will be something regal about the way we reverence each other—we will go about our homes with courtly demeanor, with an inherent love and respect for each other, radiating thoughtfulness and goodness. This King "thought it not robbery to be equal with God: but" . . . "took upon himself the form of a servant." When Christ is regnant in your heart and mine, we will be willing to serve each other. We will not always want first place, to have our considerations first, always to be "on top of the domestic pile." The moment husband or wife wishes to be superior, one to the other, a marriage becomes a competition instead of a companionship.

We must develop ourselves spiritually lest one disappoint the other. There is nothing quite so deflating as to see spiritual deficiences in one's life partner, for a man under the pressures of the hour to suddenly realize he has married a woman who has no spiritual depth. Imagine Job having suffered the loss of his sons, his property, his servants, and then his health, saying to his wife, "What shall I do now, dear?" and she replying, "Oh, I don't know. Why don't you just *'curse God and die?'* " Imagine being married to a woman whose life was stuffed with sawdust—without any spiritual resources on which a husband could draw!

On the other hand, imagine the utter disappointment of a woman who realized in an hour of trial or difficulty that she had been married to a man who had remained a "spiritual adolescent." We must not disappoint each other in the realm of religion. We shape each other's souls as wet clay is shaped and husband and wife are not the same after they have walked with each other for even a single year. It is for that reason that we are challenged constantly to a royal Christian spiritual character and demeanor, because there is no disappointment quite like that of failing to see spiritual depth in our partner and no joy equal to that of discovering it both latent and active there.

> You hold my stature. I may grow no higher
> Than you will let me, for I grow in you;
> We are but one, who first met life as two;
> I learn of loveliness as you aspire.
> If you are small, my spirit too will shrink;
> If you lack vision, then I know no goal;
> You hold the boundaries of my very soul;
> I sip the wine of living that you drink.
>
> And since you hold me in your heart's still garden,
> I cannot go unless you take my hand;
> Long have you known me, and you understand
> My urge for mountain tops. I ask no pardon
> For this strange ache to glimpse eternity.
> Love, lead the way, and make a path for me.*

A woman went to a doctor because she was on the verge of a nervous breakdown. The doctor gave her this advice, "Madam, I would advise that you spend fifteen minutes every morning in private devotion. Read your Bible for five minutes; if you don't have one, buy one. Think about what you have read for another five minutes, then talk to God for five minutes. If you don't know how to pray, learn how. You are simply God-hungry!" At this the woman became an-

* "Aspirations," by Jan Isabelle Fortune, in *Good Housekeeping*.

gry and remonstrated by saying, "I came here for physical diagnosis, not for spiritual advice." The doctor answered, "Madam, that is my diagnosis and it will cost you fifty dollars!" Angrily she stormed out of the office, but because she was desperate she tried it; her nerves quieted down, she received spiritual food, and fears stopped gnawing at her heart. There was but one difficulty with her disposition, she was God-hungry.

The hungry tiger takes it out on everyone with whom he comes in contact. You and I may do the same without that inner peace that tells us when we are right with God it will be easier to be right with other people. Your private devotions and your family altar may do more to contribute to the peace and joy of your hearthside than you quite know at this moment. Try it! Remember, as someone has said, "There is a God-shaped vacuum in everyone's heart," and until Christ is there, there will be a gnawing central emptiness somewhere in every soul.

Through all the varying scenes of life may Christ lead us and guide us. May He give us enough tears to keep us tender, enough hurts to keep us humane, enough failures to keep our hands clenched tightly in His, enough success to make us sure we march with Him, and then, when He calls us to His heavenly home, may heaven not seem far away or strange, because we have already experienced a bit of it in this earthly place that we, in God, call home.

For the kingdom of heaven is as a man traveling into a far country, who called his own servants, and delivered unto them his goods. . . . After a long time the lord of those servants cometh, and reckoneth with them.

MATTHEW *25:14, 19*

The Royal Partnership

HOW WOULD YOU FEEL IF YOU WERE ASKED TO BECOME a senior partner in the greatest business firm in the world? One whose assets were the largest in history, the powers of which are the greatest, with an area for business illimitable, and holdings beyond all precedent in history?

You are! With these words, "Seek ye first the kingdom of God, and his righteousness," you are invited into this royal partnership. The cattle on a thousand hills are God's, the forests, the fires, electricity, earth, air, herb, coin, and cataract with all its power. The operations are universal, for He said, "Go ye into all the world," as His agents and as His salesmen operating for Him. Jesus Christ is the royal Heir and Owner of this business, and Paul tells us that as we accept Him and this obligation we become "heirs" with Christ Jesus and of His riches. You and I may belong to "God and Us, Incorporated," and in our hands He has put the possessions of the universe.

Sir Walter Scott once had an estate called Abbotsford. It was necessary, however, that he often be absent from this estate on legal business in Edinburgh. During his absence, he placed his whole estate, its servants, its cattle, much of its money in the hands of Tom Purdy, who was his "steward." In that day he was called a "stigweard," "stig" standing for "sty" or "corral," in which cattle are kept, and "weard" standing for "ward," or a "keeper of the corral." After a time, Walter Scott returned and "reckoned" with Tom Purdy, asking for an accounting of all he had done with possessions, money, servants, and time.

We are ready now for our text: "For the kingdom of heaven is as a man traveling into a far country, who called his own servants, and delivered unto them his goods. . . . After a long time the lord of those servants cometh, and reckoned with them." May I paraphrase that? For the kingdom of this world, the Kingdom of God, is likened unto Christ who co-created it and co-owns it with the Father. He has called us all unto Him and given unto some of us five talents; to others, two and to others, one, and is now at the right hand of God. Some day He will come and reckon with us, asking for an account of all we have done with that which He placed in our hands.

Let us glance at the kingly principles in this thrilling business with God.

In the first place, let us remember that *all we have is God's;* He is the Creator of fire, wood, steel, fruit, minerals, land. When I was a boy we used to play "real estate" by getting some white balls of grocery twine from my mother's kitchen drawer and, with clothespins, marked off my father's backyard into plots. We then called in the neighboring children and pretended to sell these plots for a penny—until my mother discovered it and made us return the pennies! The land, of course, was still my father's. There are a lot of men today simply playing "real estate"—the land belongs to God. We pretend to own it and we pretend to sell it; we die and leave it to someone else; but we are developed by "playing the game." The only difference between men and boys is that a man's toys cost more!

God, the great Owner, gives us certain principles for paying and giving, even as a government regiments what we do with a portion of our possessions. If we withhold from the government what properly belongs to it, we find ourselves in jail. We withhold certain moneys that belong to God and no drastic action is taken. Once in a while God shows His anger at poor stewardship, such as toward Ananias and Sapphira, when both of them dropped dead for financial misrepresentation in the church. But I am afraid that if that

93

should happen today there would be a good many funerals after an every-member canvass. The punishment for the careless handling of money, in the realm of the spirit, comes to us in different ways, even as His rewards come to us in different ways.

This partnership with God should start with a *definite portion*. God's early system called for a portion, or a tithe, a tenth, to be set apart in recognition of the fact that all man had was God's. The tithe is not particularly Jewish, for the patriarchs—Jacob and others—practiced it before there was a nation of Israel. It was simply "interest" on the "loan" of what God had given them. We do not "pay" a bank or "make a gift" to that bank when we pay "interest." God is the Banker. He makes us His loan and He asks for interest on the loan.

There are decided benefits in definite proportionate giving. First of all, it keeps us from being dishonest without knowing it. God told Malachi to say that Israel had "robbed him in tithes and offerings." A "tithe" is a tenth, and the "offering" is that amount *above the tithe,* which depends upon both our generosity and our abilities; but a tithe is not a "gift," it is only a "payment of interest." This sort of system, of proportionate giving, also safeguards our stewardship. One woman said, "I believe that if I should really keep books I would find that I not only give a tenth but that I give even as much as a twentieth!"

These businesslike payments of a definite proportion are very important but often neglected. A Federal agent once called at the home of a certain man and informed him that he was "under arrest." The man remonstrated that he had been a good husband and had supported his wife, in which his wife concurred. Also, that he had supported his children well, paid his grocery bills at the corner grocery store, and had also paid his doctor's bills. The Federal agent said, "I'm not arresting you for not paying your debts to these persons, I am arresting you for income tax evasion. You did not pay the proper amount to the Federal government." Remember that the Kingdom of God is the "Federal government" of God. It may be perfectly possible that you and I on the horizontal should pay our debts to wife and children, to groceryman and doctor, and then on the perpendicular cheat the kingdom of God, His church, and the spiritual economy.

After we have decided on a definite proportion, there is the challenge of the *sliding scale*. The government thinks that is legitimate, and the larger the income, the larger the percentage we pay to the government. This should also be God's economy—"as God hath prospered us." The larger our income, the less percentage we need for ourselves and the larger the percentage we should be pleased and privileged to give to spiritual things. Zacchæus was prosperous enough to say, "Half of all I have will I give to the poor." He was able to give fifty per cent because he could live on fifty per cent. There were times in the Old Testament history when the Jews added certain offerings to their tithe and gave as much as thirty per cent. A late president of a great railroad gave as much as eighty-five per cent of his income to God, feeling that he could live on fifteen per cent.

But how much do we need for ourselves? The pity is that so many people lay up "treasure for themselves." A seaman prayed one night at a meeting of sailors, "Lord, make us ships with two hatches, please. One to take in the cargo, and the other to give it out." You and I are all ships engaged in the heavenly commerce, loaded with gifts by God, and we must make delivery for Him. Paul said, "I have received of the Lord that which I also delivered unto you," and that which we receive, we should deliver again to the service of God.

Some people think it is necessary to keep up with the Jones—but why should you want to keep up with the Jones? Do you know where they are going? How would you like to be with the Jones one hundred years from now? It might be a very commendable situation, and yet again it might not be! It is so easy for us to want to "get ahead of our neighbors and acquaintances."

The main aim in your life and mine should be, not to keep up with the Jones but to keep up with

Christ and His kingdom and be sure that it may never bog down.

When it comes to the right Christian standard of living it is somewhat difficult to ascertain. What do we mean by "self-denial" today? Do we mean the denial of St. Francis of Assisi? Or of a great musician who said that he hesitated to buy an expensive meal because in doing so he felt he was robbing the poor? Our Christian spending need not be placed on the "false premise that material things are evil in themselves." Nor need we base it on the mistaken idea that pain, privation, famine, and a lack of things are particularly spiritual conditions. God wants us to have the comforts of life and enough. He said, "Seek ye first the kingdom of God, and his righteousness, and all these things"—what you eat and drink, and wear— "shall be added unto you." God wants us to have these things, but we should be careful that we do not pile luxury on luxury and that our selfish indulgence does not become habitual. One man said, "When I reached the point where I had a surplus over my needs in my income, I decided to give as much to God as I spent on myself and family, so I called in my minister one day and I said, 'I am buying a new car; it costs so much. Here is a check for the same amount for Christ.' " A month or so later, he said, "We are putting an extension on our house. We don't really need it, but we would like it and it would add to our comfort, so here is a check to match the cost of the extension we are building. We don't propose to spend more on our own pleasure than we spend on God's. God gave us everything we have."

There are two questions that have to do with saving. First of all, *"How much shall we save?"* Of course, hoarding can have no place in the Christian's life; the miser is a vanishing man. The government sees to that, but it is permissible for us to save something. Let God tell us how much. It is the purpose of saving that is important. There was a certain man called the "Miser of Marseilles." Everybody considered him very grasping. One day he died, and everybody said, "The skinflint is dead." But they bit their lips, for the next day his will was published and this vast amount of money was left in order that water might be piped into the public square in the city of Marseilles, that all the thirsty might have water free. He had saved to serve!

A great many people miss the joy of giving while they are still alive and can enjoy its results. "We shall receive a reward for deeds *done in the flesh.*" "In the flesh" means while we are still alive. There is an adage that says, "What we give to God in our health is gold; what we give in our sickness is silver; but what we give in death is lead." This, probably, because it is no sacrifice to leave it behind, since we cannot take it with us.

We should look to our wills, too. The Christian should never leave a pagan will. There should be some evidence in it, as people read it, that we realized that we were here on business for the King, because the will we leave is the last thing we say about God, about Christ, in this world.

There is a danger here in this kingdom business. It is that we feel that our stewardship is less important because we have little to handle. One may die from a fall from a five-hundred-foot cliff as easily as from a five-thousand-foot cliff. The careless handling of an allowance of ten dollars a month might be just as spiritually disastrous as the mishandling of ten thousand dollars a month. It is not the *force* of what we have but the *faithfulness* with which we handle it. Small amounts well-handled may also bring us thrilling results. The lord would have commended the one-talent man for proper use of his single talent with exactly the same words with which he commended the five-talent man. The sunlight that comes through a single pinprick in a piece of paper is the same pure sunlight that comes pouring through a spacious glass window. There is as much glory in using small possessions well as in using immense possessions well.

God always has His present-day rewards for good business relationships with Himself on the part of His people. "All thou spendest, Jesus will repay."

During the Civil War a messenger, riding into

99

the home town of General Stonewall Jackson, deposited a letter from the general in the hand of the pastor. An anxious crowd gathered on the church steps as the letter was opened, expecting news of the war—Missionary Ridge or Lookout Mountain. But the letter read: "My dear Pastor: I recalled today that my gift to foreign missions was due. Find it enclosed. May the day soon come when this war is over, and may the right side win, that we may go back to our primary task of saving the souls of men." If we had been busy at our primary task, if we have invested in "saving the souls of men" as much as we have in slaying men, this world would have been far ahead.

Because we put only two billion dollars into changing the hearts of men in a single year, we shall be spending fifty billion dollars into putting guns in their hands. I would be willing spiritually to wager this: that if we would double our gifts to missions, religion and the changing of hearts of people, for five successive years, we would cut down our war bill from fifty billion to twenty-five billion and thus be better bankers by twenty-five billion dollars and call our dear lads home. But we seem not to learn!

The same thing is true of the *rewards of tomorrow* in this thrilling business. Remember, when you give to God and spiritual things, you are not giving, you are really "depositing"—"laying up treasure for yourselves in heaven." What you and I keep, we lose. What we have given away we keep forever.

There is the story of a certain woman who was visiting heaven; a woman who had been of considerable means on earth. She passed a rather modest bungalow and she said rather lightly to St. Peter, "And whose bungalow is this?" He said, "That is yours, madam." Rather disappointed, they walked on, and she spied a large estate, a costly mansion, and said, "And whose is this?" He said, "That estate belongs to Harry Smith." "Strange," she said, "Harry Smith was the name of my chauffeur." He said, "That's right. It is Harry Smith's. You see, madam, in building the mansions here in heaven, we have only such material to use in their building as is sent up to us. Such material as is given to God. This mansion represents what Harry Smith sent up, and the bungalow what you sent up." She awoke with a start!

Remember, my friends, you cannot take it with you but you can send it ahead.

These things write I unto thee . . . , that thou mayest know how men ought to behave themselves in the house of God, which is the church of the living God, . . . the pillar and ground of the truth.

I TIMOTHY *3:14, 15*

The Etiquette of the Kingdom

ONE OF THE MANY TRAGEDIES OF THE LAST WAR WAS the death, or the near death, of one of society's greatest virtues—courtesy. It has largely gone from the market place—from both sides of the counter. It has disappeared from three-quarters of our public dining-rooms and from a large percentage of our domestic dining-rooms as well. Doors are now slammed in your faces, men's hats are glued to their heads, and many women have forgotten how to say "thank you."

The story is told of a certain man who, seeing a woman standing in a streetcar, rose to give her his seat. She was so astonished at the courtesy that she fell over in a faint. When they revived her, seeing the man who had shown her the courtesy, she said, "Thank you, sir." The man, in turn, was so astonished that he dropped dead. It is a humorous story illustrating a tragic decay.

A young naval officer just about to sit down in one

of a pair of empty seats in a motion picture theatre was abruptly pushed aside by a woman, with her husband trailing behind her. Before the officer could recover, the couple had plumped down into the two seats with a "Sorry, my friend," from the husband, "we beat you." "That is all right," said the officer, "I hope you and your mother enjoy the show."

Courtesy has been defined as that essential characteristic of a gentleman which enables him at all times to put himself in the place of others and to be devoid of any action from which he himself would recoil.

But what has etiquette to do with this series of discussions on "The Kingdom of God"? The Holy Spirit has thought it important enough to enter a discussion of it in His sacred pages. Paul, writing to young Timothy, the pastor of the church at Ephesus, admonishes him and his followers that they "know how men ought to behave themselves in the house of God, which is the church of the living God." The church is God's household of faith. It is the duty of each member of it to extend to the other the royal family courtesies. The children of the King should act like Him. Those who have been adopted into the family of God, through Christ, should conduct themselves as those whose escutcheon and coat-of-arms belong to royalty. If we are spiritually regenerated it should show itself in our behavior. If we are made "nigh by the blood of Christ," then let us make sure that "blood will tell."

They captured a Highland lad with royal blood in his veins and endeavored to disguise him by dressing him in homespun, but he could not belie his training and was discovered—kings' sons do not eat potatoes with knives. It is not enough that you and I should be spiritual "diamonds in the rough"—we should be polished by the Holy Spirit.

God is easily "grieved" by the lack of decorum. In Ephesians 4:30 Paul has reminded us that we should "grieve not the Holy Spirit," as He is very sensitive to some un-Christian traits. What attributes of character had Paul mentioned in the preceding verses?—greediness, careless conversation, bad temper, haste, and other weaknesses so common in the characters of today.

Let us, then, mention briefly some of the principles of conduct that are necessary to the warmth, the culture, the joy and the dignity of God's household of faith. In the Old Testament, Uzziah was stricken with leprosy because of the violation of certain temple etiquettes. Two other young men were struck dead because they behaved themselves carelessly at the altars of God's House.

These are the days of the New Testament and grace. But if fear does not make us careful, love certainly will, and there are principles of kingly courtesy that will ever point us out among the crowd.

Let the first of these be a *courteous answer to the King's invitation*—"Enter into his gates with thanksgiving, and into his courts with praise," . . . "not forsaking the assembling of ourselves together." God has a right to our worship. It is as meat to His soul and food to His heart. It is certainly His due, and yet it might surprise you to know that only twenty-four per cent of the Christians were in any church this morning and that only five per cent will worship God at eventide in His sanctuary. There are such cruel neglects of this invitation to His house. Our church attendance is so easily defeated; it is beaten to death with golf clubs; we sleep on Sunday mornings; friends drop in to defeat His invitation, and rather than hurt their feelings we hurt God's and deny ourselves the privilege of His presence. Nations always pay for absence from the house of God.

There will also be the holy *etiquette of prayer*. Think of it—the breath-taking consciousness that when we pray we are ushered into the throne room of God, given audience by the King of the universe, receiving His ear for moments upon moments, having ready access to Him through intercession. This is one of the most remarkable benefits offered those who belong to the household of God.

I have had conversation with certain women who have been presented to the Queen of England, and I have sensed something of the awe, the demeanor, the careful deportment, the training, before they were ushered in to her august presence. It should be no little thing to have speech with God. We should not clutter up our prayers with useless chatter; we should endeavor to think on at length; we should make our requests as regal and as thoughtful as possible, and all this should be done with a sense of unusual privilege.

One of the most impolite things that we can do is not to allow the other person in a conversation to have a part. I knew one woman, who, whenever she called me on the telephone, ran along for minutes, her conversation being a "river of words and a trickle of mind." I knew there was no chance of my cutting in at all, even with a rapidly gasped suggestion. She always monopolized the conversation. How many of us pray like that? We do all the speaking, and God has no chance to even answer back. When we have finished our verbal portrayals of our wishes, our problems, and our wills, most of us are up from our knees swiftly, and God has no chance to reply. This sort of praying in one direction, this sort of *monologue,* in which we speak to God, instead of *dialogue,* in which we allow Him also to speak to us, has its roots in spiritual egotism. It is just one quiet way of saying impolitely that what we have to tell God is far more important than what God has to tell us.

Remember that in prayer the ear is just as important as the tongue—more so, because the King has so much to tell His subjects.

It is evident that Paul thinks that the *etiquette of dress* is pertinent. Someone has said that your dress is your "table of contents."

Paul says, "Let women *adorn* themselves." That is a part of the commandment. We are not of more value in the realm of Kingdom influences when we go about dressed dowdily and "down at the heel." No woman has any right to look as beautiful as Venus as she goes to the marriage altar and then become careless and slovenly and, after six months, look like a witch. We should look our best—it is our duty to God.

Let all women "adorn themselves in *modest apparel*." There is a modesty, too, that is beautiful and acceptable in the realm of the Kingdom.

One evening a young woman was waiting for a young man to come and take her out. As she sat in the easy chair in her parlor she looked at herself in her new evening gown; then she stared! She went upstairs, changed her dress, came down, looking beautiful but different!

> If Christ should come today to visit me,
> And sit awhile in the chair before the fire
> That always is reserved for company—
> I think that I would hide my nakedness.
> I think my cheeks would burn a deeper shade
> Of red than they were rouged, and I would bite

108

My sticky, carmined lips, and be afraid
Mascaraed lashes really held a lure.
I think before He ever spoke a word
About the sunny weather, or had asked
If all were well—I think I would have heard
My guilty heart protest its innocence.
But not for long, because I know that I
Would fall before His feet, and I would ask
Forgiveness for my sins, and I would cry:
"Have mercy, O thou holy Son of God!" *

I am not discussing mascaraed lashes or rouged lips; I do not think that they have anything to do particularly with morality. I am just talking about the effect some people try to have.

Two men looked out through prison bars,
One saw mud, the other saw stars!

I wonder what would happen if all Christian womanhood dressed for the eyes of Christ. I know that they would appear as beautiful as possible, but that is not all.

The same thing is true of men. A British peer once said, "Dress has a moral effect upon the conduct of mankind. Let any gentleman find himself with dirty boots, soiled neckerchief and a general negligence of dress and he will find a corresponding negligence of address."

He was a British official. A friend burst into his

* "Lenten Meditation," by Mildred Allen Jeffery.

African hut and saw him there, ludicrously sitting in a dinner jacket with all the appointments of a formal dinner, waited upon by some African savages. "Harry," he said, "have you gone crazy? Dressing for dinner among a lot of African natives?" To this the British official replied, "Sir, I belong to the British Empire. There is a certain something that is England and I do not want to forget it. If I did not dress for dinner once a week, I would soon be conducting myself like these African hottentots that are all about me." That is the trouble with a lot of us. In our deportment we do not care to "dress for dinner," we do not want to "high-hat" our friends by higher actions and habits of Christian standards, so we lay aside the dress suit of Christian morals and we go about in "moral negligee," plunging ourselves down to the cheap level of the African hottentots who are all about us in a decadent society.

There is the etiquette of *social warmth.* This is a cold world in which we live. The Church of Jesus Christ should be a warm fireplace. A young man went into a lapidary shop and said to the jeweler, "I want to see your finest opal for the finest woman in the world." To this the jeweler replied, "I have the opal, you have the lady; let us get them together." He brought out the opal and placed it in the prospective customer's hand. The customer asked, "How much is this?" "Seven hundred dollars." The man said, "My friend, I am not buying a diamond. I'm purchasing an opal." The jeweler smiled, "That is a very famous opal, sir." "But," remonstrated the customer, "there is no fire in it. It seems milky, dead." The jeweler said, "Give me the stone." He took the stone and cupped it in the palm of his hand, closed his fingers over it and allowed the warmth of those fingers to saturate the stone, then opening his fingers, displayed the opal. It was flashing fire, and the jeweler explained, "This is one of the most famous hand opals in the world. It never flashes its fire until it feels the warmth of a human hand." How true that is. There are many people outside of the kingdom who are listless, fireless as far as spiritual heat is concerned—utterly listless so far as God is concerned—but they would flash fire if only they felt the warmth of a human hand!

One man, when asked why he accepted Christ and joined the church, said, "It was one pound's pressure on my coat lapel in the narthex of your church, placed there by a businessman. I had waited seven years for that!" How many men have been lost to the Kingdom enterprise for the lack of one pound's pressure on their coat lapels?

A certain man, returning from a large city church in which he had received no warmth of welcome, was asked by his wife the subject of the sermon. It happened that the minister had used as his text, "Many are called but few are chosen." The man's comment was,

"I don't know. It was something like 'Many were cold
and a few were frozen!' " The Kingdom of God cannot
let its fires of concern go out in a chilling hour like
this. Jesus Christ is the light of the world, and where
there is light, there should be warmth; where there is
warmth, there will be people.

Let us also recognize that part of Kingdom etiquette which is the *lack of haste*. "Let not thine heart
be hasty." We are seldom socially impressed with people who cannot "be bothered with us"—who are always
in a hurry. In the fulness of time, God sent forth His
Son—how patient God had been waiting for men
through the centuries to give due recognition to Him,
His love, and His kingdom, and now, at long last,
Christ came. Time seemed no element with Him—He
gave it lavishly to us, He spent his days healing men,
His nights talking to Nicodemus and others about their
doubts; He gave up His luncheon hour to speak to a
woman at the well about her soul, used His nights in
praying for you and me, walked all the way to Bethany
to attend a funeral and to break it up, spent long hours
on a cross, and three days in a tomb waiting to rise for
our justification, and is now spending all of His time
"making intercession for us" at the throne of God.
All of His time is ours. How much of our time is His?
Folks used to have considerable time for God and sermons in the colonial days. Sermons were often two-
and-a-half or three hours long and "irksome only to

the ungodly." After a minister had preached for three hours, a young man came up to him and said, "You tired me out—you preached too long." The preacher gave the young man a withering look and said, "Young man, you're a little jug and you are very easily filled." We are! We become jumpy when prayers are more than three minutes long. We want "sermonettes by preacherettes." We want everything boiled down. We are in a desperate hurry. We waste time *that belongs to God,* and because of this our souls go hungry, remain immature, and suffer from spiritual malnutrition.

I have written to him the great things of my law, but they were counted as a strange thing.

The Kingly Letter

HOSEA WAS OF A NATION THAT WAS ABOUT TO "CRACK up," in which all the elements of destruction lay in hiding and were not being corrected. But I want to choose one thing of these various weaknesses that could mark any nation's downfall—it was the tragedy of an *unopened letter,* a nation's neglect of the Word of God.

The words in our text were spoken to Ephraim. The Bible of his day was incomplete—yet rich in content, but he had neglected it. Dust was on the parchments. He was not familiar with what was in them. The message from God lay unopened; a King's commands lay unheeded, His plan unworked. God was grieved both because of what Ephraim was missing and because of what his nation was missing.

I want to talk to you about your Bible.

First of all, remember the Author. "*I* have written to him." God has written a kingly letter to you and to me. We should have suspected that. Some sort of a Bible is a necessity. God must reveal His will somewhere and explain His heart to men. If He is Judge of the world, He must give us laws to follow; if He is the way, He must explain that way and place in our hands a spiritual map. If He is our Father, He must have counsel with us; if we are made in His image and have the capacity to understand Him, then there must be the means of understanding Him. And here it is. "All scripture given by inspiration of God is profitable for doctrine, for reproof, for correction, for instruction in righteousness."

"But," you say, "men wrote it." That is true, but they wrote as God's tools; they were not the actual authors of what they wrote. The Bible "came not of old by the will of man." It is true that writers like Matthew, Mark, Luke, John, and the prophets wrote through their own personalities and colored what they said with their own style, but they never claimed authorship. They felt they were but the vehicles through which God moved. The truths which they wrote were far beyond the limits of their own minds to invent, and on every page of the Holy Writ you may well write these words, "Thus saith the Lord."

In this the Bible is different from any other literature. Inspiration means to "inbreathe." The Bible is literature "inbreathed" by the Holy Spirit. A professor of biology held a little brown seed in his hand. He

116

said, "I know just exactly the composition of this seed. It has in it hydrogen, carbon, nitrogen. I can make a seed exactly like this seed that I hold in my hand, but the seed I would make and plant lacks what we call the 'life principle.' The seed I would make would rot and die, but the seed God made gives life and reproduces itself." The Bible has in it the "life principle." Simply plant it in your heart and see what happens. That will prove the divine authorship of the book. Let a man read it, it will lead him to God; let a man study it, he will know the heart of God. Let a man ask his questions and he will find his answers. Let him test the Christ of these pages and he will find the power that Christ has to give.

The fact that this is God's kingly letter to you should make a difference—if you love Him. A young man called on a woman of whom he was very fond, left in her hands a manuscript, and asked her to peruse it. Coming back a day or two later, he said, "How did you like the story?" She said, "I thought it was boring, dull and impossibly dry." He colored somewhat and said, "Well, you know, I wrote that." She said, "Oh, I'm sorry. Let me have it; I shall read it again." The next time he came back, she was radiant. She said, "It is a thrilling story." When we love an author it opens our eyes to certain splendors. If you love God, His letter will not lie unopened on the table. Your heart will reach out for it avidly and with new interest, for the will of God to you is everything.

Again, may I remind you of *the great price* at which this letter was delivered to you? It came through by registered mail, stamped with men's blood. Prophets died for their pains, some of them for penning it, others suffered martyrdom. They were driven into the caves and rocks; they became men without a country, chased by kings and peasants, rich and poor, bond and free. The man who carried the message to Garcia underwent only part of the travail that those who penned these lines for God suffered. Tradition says that Matthew was beaten to death by a fuller's club. Mark was martyred in the eighth year of Nero; Luke wrote his gospel and was slain under Domitian; Paul wrote his epistles, and was beheaded at Three Fountains at Rome; Peter wrote and was crucified head downward for his audacity of tongue and pen.

The modern translation of your Bible was placed in your hands by those who came through the fires. They translated it in dungeons; they wrote under pain of death. Jerome translated the Latin Vulgate and was sorely persecuted; Luther translated the Bible for the German masses and had to hide away in Wartburg Castle, in danger of his life. Tyndale made a translation for English hearts and went to a martyr's death, crying, "Lord, open the eyes of the King of England!" Coverdale couched these truths for the Anglo-Saxon mind and he too perished. It cost a great deal, my friend, to post and carry this letter to you. Since that day, emissaries and missionaries of God have carried it through giant forests and steaming jungles to all races of men. The Bible that lies within reach of your hand at this hour has been distributed by men with wills of steel and hearts with a sense of empire as broad as this world. The American Bible Society, which we salute today on this "Bible Sunday," has translated the Bible in innumerable languages at the cost of millions of dollars and at great personal sacrifice. Humanity will never be able to repay this great organization born in the heart of God for the lamps it has lighted in the souls of men, for the printed promises it has carried to the dark places, and for the white cloths on its pages on which so many have blotted and dried their tears.

beautiful

Let us rehearse briefly some of the majestic treasures that lie bound within the covers of this book.

Here we have the kingly *laws of God*. We shall all be "judged by the word of this law." Here are the commandments of God and the edicts of the Almighty for the human race. "These things that I speak unto you, the same shall judge you in the last day." Ignorance of these laws will be no excuse. When one takes the wheel of a car he must know the rules of the highways and the roads. Ignorance of these laws of traffic is no excuse, and when you and I take over the wheel of life we should know the laws governing the highways of God and society. The failure to read does not excuse us.

Here, too, is a thrilling *plan for your life.* For what am I living? This is the "sixty-four-dollar question" of life. God, why was I created? For God's glory. Why does a man live? For me to live is Christ. What is the supreme purpose of my life? To seek first the Kingdom of God and His righteousness. Where am I going? Here are your thrilling plans for the future. Here we are warned against false goals in life. Against living for pleasure alone—"She that liveth for pleasure is dead while she liveth." Of merely amassing things—"A man's life consisteth not in the abundance of the things which he possesseth." Money?—"Lay not up for yourself treasures on earth." Self?—"Seekest thou great things for thy self? Seek them not." Physical desires?—"Live not after the flesh but after the spirit."

Here, too, is a *stage* where living examples walk before us with their startling and thrilling admonition: Cain to counsel with you about the danger of jealousy. Judas to warn you against the love of money. The sons of Elihu to warn us against disobedience. Pilate to show us how it never pays to live for the crowd or to follow the mores of public opinion. David to challenge you with the love of God. Moses to call you to faith, and Christ to show you the glory of the Father.

Here is a *correcting guide.* You cannot always

trust conscience in a day like this. True, some people follow their conscience as they follow a wheelbarrow; they push it around wherever they want it to go. Conscience needs the "sun observation" of God's word. You can usually set your watch by the chronometer in the jewelry store window, but sometimes beside that chronometer there may rest a card saying, "This chronometer is so many seconds slow or fast by Greenwich Prime Meridian reading, sun observation." Even the chronometer must be corrected. We can often run the watch of our lives by the chronometer of conscience. Sometimes conscience itself must be corrected by sun observation, which is the word of God.

Here, too, in this letter is a *pattern for character*. Here is the highest good, the moral ultimate of your life. Jesus Christ said, "He that hath seen me, hath seen the Father." "Follow me." British scientists, many years ago, did an almost perfect work in fashioning the most perfect yardstick in the world. It is made of platinum and iridium, and has become the standard of the British government. Every ten years it is examined, and if it varies one-thousandth of an inch it will be rejected. It still stands. Here is the great rule of faith and practice for human life—the yardstick of character and career.

Here, too, is *an accurate photograph* of your character and mine. We might not like it—this full-length portrait of ourselves which we see mirrored in these pages. We might have conceived ourselves to be swans and find ourselves to be ugly ducklings in the realm of the spirit. Sinful men, once satisfied with reading this book, will turn to God with a new sense of need. People who thought they amounted to nothing will here have their worth explained. Men who stumbled and thought they could never rise again will find in these pages new hope for their sins, though they be as scarlet. Folks who have lost their star will find it again as a hunter comes on a lost trail.

Let us make this letter practical as we read it. Your body lives by two processes, *assimilation and elimination*—taking in and giving out. The soul will grow by the same two processes. Read a few verses of the Word of God—not too many—then stop and ask this question, "God, what is in these verses that you commend? Is that in my life? If not, help me take it in now." That is assimilation. Ask, then, "God, what is in these verses that you condemn? Is that in my life? Help me to put it out now." That is elimination. By these two processes your soul will grow and the Bible will suddenly become fascinating in its application.

Here, too, is the King's letter about *your future*. It is thrilling to know that the Christian is the only one who knows his future. All other plans of "mice and men gang agley." About tomorrow, God everywhere speaks with certainty and surety. The ship of humanity might at times seem to be in a bad way, but above the fog God stands on the bridge of providence, and He will see us through, for His eyes are above the fogs of human history and caprice. Here is your promise of eternal life. Spiritual things are "spiritually discerned." You cannot scan the heavens with the naked eye; the telescope will reveal the existence of planets unseen by your normal sight. His word places a telescope to your eye, and you can see the heavenly truths that would be undiscovered by your unaided intellect. This is a day in which we need not only the *reason of man* but also the *revelation of God*.

When nine Dartmouth College men were found dead in their beds by asphyxiation in their fraternity house, you can imagine that at the funeral services two thousand student hearts were as tense as harpstrings when the president said:

At a time like this, this college is most effectively shorn of its affectations, its petty poses and its specious sophistries. We see life in its great dimensions. We begin to sense that rationalism is not all and that there is no harder or colder form of materialism than the materialism of pure intellect untempered by the influence of heart and soul. We begin to understand assertions like that of Aubrey L. Moore, the brilliant young English essayist, "that human nature claims to be both rational and religious and the life that is not both is neither!"

A soldier was dying on the field of battle, the chaplain was bending over him, and the soldier gasped,

"Give me a light, Chaplain." The chaplain reached into the soldier's pocket, took out a cigarette, put it between his lips, and was about to strike the match when the soldier said, "The other kind of light, Chaplain." The chaplain reached into his pocket, took out a Testament, and began to read. "Let not your heart be troubled: ye believe in God, believe also in me. In my father's house are many mansions." The soldier sighed, "That's it, Chaplain," and with that he died. What do men do in the shadows without this light?

How will the guesses of men ever arm us with the surety we need as we look ahead? There is a verse that says, so far as the future is concerned, "Eye hath not seen . . . ," that is, science cannot prove eternal life. "Ear hath not heard"—there is no personal testimony of any who have returned from the far-off country. "Neither hath entered into the mind of man, the things which God hath prepared for them that love him," that is, you cannot merely with the tools of philosophy and reason conjure up full proofs for eternal life. "But," Paul goes on to say, "God hath revealed them unto us by his Spirit: for the Spirit searcheth all things, yea, the deep things of God. For we know that, if our earthly house of this tabernacle were dissolved we have a building of God, an house not made with hands, eternal in the heavens." This is a revelation of the spirit written on the sacred pages of the King's letter, without which we subtract from our lives the great convictions of tomorrow and the day after to-morrow.

A university student stepped up to me once and said, "You know, Dr. Evans, I have always thanked God that He has trained the diaphragm of the camera of my mind to take a long, long shot!"

Let it never be said of us as it was said of Ephraim, "I have written to him the great things of my law but they are as a strange thing unto him."

Opening this kingly letter, devouring it with eager heart, and following its precepts in regal life, let us be able to say as David said, "Oh, how I love thy law. It is my meditation all the day long."

The government shall be upon his shoulder.

ISAIAH *9:6*

The kingdoms of this world are become the kingdoms of our Lord, and of his Christ; and he shall reign for ever and ever.

REVELATION *11:15*

The Kingly Vision

THESE ARE THRILLING WORDS AS WE APPROACH CHRIST-
mas. There is no room in Christianity for small minds,
it challenges people to a sense of empire. This is the
cry of Christendom:

> Bring me men to match my mountains,
> Bring me men to match my plains,
> Men with empires in their purpose,
> And new eras in their brains.*

When you and I step into Christendom, when you and
I follow Jesus Christ, we become a part of a great imperial, majestic program to make Christ King of kings
and Lord of lords. Charlemagne, Cæsar, Hannibal,
and Napoleon never dreamed of the breath-taking con-
summation of power that Christ prophesied for Himself when He said "My kingdom." None of these
rulers or partial rulers of the hearts of men ever fashioned a song with this breadth and majesty,

* Sam Walter Foss, from "The Coming American."

From Greenland's icy mountains,
From India's coral strand,
Where Afric's sunny fountains
Roll down their golden sand. . . .*

At Christmas Christ "came unto his own, and his own received him not." "Without him was nothing made that was made." The world was rightly His. The terrestrial ball of this world, in all of its disobedience, had rolled out of the garden of God; Christ at Christmas came to retrieve that ball and place it back in the hand of God, where it has always belonged.

That is the fundamental purpose of our lives. To this cause we were all born: "Seek ye first the kingdom of God, and his righteousness," and bring the world back to Him again.

This passion seized the Early Church in the first century. It grew by leaps and bounds. Peter, after a vision on a house top, hurried out to bring other races to the footstool of Christ and he met his death in far-off Rome. John sailed away to uncharted places. Tradition tells us that Matthew made his way to India and blazed a trail. Paul stalked off with confidence to Athens and Corinth and on Mars Hill he spoke with a sense of empire. The medieval centuries saw the spread of the Christian gospel through the Mediterranean and Asia Minor; then the Druids of the British Isles stopped worshiping their idols and began to sing

* Bishop Reginald Heber, the Presbyterian Hymnal.

their hymns. The virile message traveled like wild-fire.

In modern times the same sense of empire revived. Carey made his way to an unknown country. Paton went to the New Hebrides. Livingstone blazed the way of empire in the jungles of Africa. Grenfell carried his ensign to the frozen Arctic wastes of Labrador.

Men shouted, "Give me the whole Bible for my faith, Christ for my Saviour, the whole Church for my fellowship, and a whole world for my parish."

Paul began as a dynamic layman when once Christ had captured him. In Romans the first chapter, he gives us the three motivating forces of the powerful spiritual life—three great principles and preparations that will seize your heart and mind in this strategic day of empire if we are the King's men and women.

"*I am not ashamed* of the gospel of Christ." Search where you will, there is no other solution for the pains and problems of the universe but Jesus of Nazareth. Having tried everything else, we have come back to Jesus Christ through the process of elimination. I lunched with Dr. William Lyon Phelps of Yale University shortly before his death and thrillingly heard him reiterate the supremacy of Jesus Christ in the midst of the needs of this world. You remember that he said, "Jesus knew more about political economy than all the professors in all the colleges in the world, and He knew more about the human heart than Shakespeare. While I am not sure of many things I am just as sure as I stand here that Jesus is the greatest Leader, the most absolutely right Person the world has ever known. . . . I am not out of my mind when I say that the only way the world can be saved today is by following Jesus Christ."

With this thrilling confidence in the Son of God, let us carry Him to the far corners of the earth.

In the second place, Paul also said, *"I am a debtor."* A tremendous responsibility attaches itself to having the Light. If we place the candle under a bushel one of two things happen, either the light goes out or the bushel is consumed. It is no small crime to withhold helpful information from folks who need it, to keep silent the name of the physician who could give the thrilling cure, not to point the way of escape to those who are imprisoned, or to fail to hand the key of deliverance to those who are in the dungeons of habit and wrong. It is no little thing for the watchman to fail to warn of the approach of an enemy or to let men know how they may have exemption for themselves from the entanglements of habit, sin and wrong, when the solution is apparent. Christianity is something you cannot keep unless you share, and a Christ unshared is a Christ lost to the individual that fails to share Him.

The command, "Go ye into all the world," makes us immediately debtors to all mankind. If we do not go in person, we must go in purse, and we must go in prayer, for this is our task—to bring this world back to Him.

A great general in World War II reminded us that the Pacific war was a "theological war." The religious conception of Amatarasu, the Sun Goddess, was never adequate for the Japanese; only now that we have preached to them the Fatherhood of God as it is in Jesus Christ have they begun to have the vision that can spell all-world brotherhood and sorority.

What we have stated before is again relevant here. All the military can do is by force to strap the conquered nations to the table—Japan, Germany, and some of the rest of them. All the military does is "administer the anesthetic." It is up to the Christian people to move in as the physicians of the spirit and perform the spiritual therapeutic so needed; it is for them to come in and remove the cancerous feelings, the diseased portions of the mind, to substitute the right theology for a bad theology, the right concepts for the evil concepts. Unless the Christian forces of the world do this, when the patients—the nations—convalesce, these will be the same as before we "knocked them out" by military anesthetic. Fools we are to spend a trillion dollars the world around for the anesthetic and then fail to perform the operation on the souls of men. We would not spend ten thousand dollars to build a chapel or a little school to change the thinking of Japan, so we spent ten million dollars on a cruiser. What poor bankers we are! Would you like to do that again? Take your choice.

Your sons and mine will go abroad some day, either with guns or with God, with bombs or with Bibles, with battleships or brotherhood—take your choice. But when Christ said, "Go ye into all the world, and preach the gospel to every creature," He was recommending to you and me the most economical, the wisest thing that civilization can do.

For not with swords loud clashing, nor roll of stirring drums,
But deeds of love and mercy, God's heavenly Kingdom comes.*

With this sense of empire, Paul also said, "I am ready." We are face to face with the ghastly truth that we are not ready or prepared to build a Christian empire. Our theological seminaries should now be as plentifully manned and filled with young cadets of the spirit as our West Point and Annapolis. Our budgets for preparation for this great capturing of the citadels of the hearts of men should be as adequate as the budgets for other sorts of campaigns. Someone asked Queen Victoria how long it would take for the British army and navy to carry a message throughout all the world. She said, "Thirty days." We have been at this since the command of Christ, "Go ye into all

* "Lead On, O King Eternal," Presbyterian Hymnal.

132

the world, and preach the gospel to every creature," and two thousand years have passed and still the greater portion of the world has never heard. With courage a few Christians walked into China, but with half-hearted home logistics we failed to support them properly. We made only a partial advance. Then came the Communists—their youth schooled in the religion of the sickle, with Marxian philosophy, and with an intoxicating love for Stalin and the Cause. In seven and a half years they swept China! They were prepared with a budget of mind and in soul for that conflict. You and I will never win the world for that which is Christian until a passion seizes our hearts as we follow the sign of the cross—a passion that is greater than those who follow the sign of the sickle. We will have to more than equal Communism in our personal sacrifices, in the availability of our persons, our purses, our possessions, our programs, and our powers. We have been trifling with this aim of "the world for Christ." We have not gone into all the world and "preached" in missionary formation, we have merely gone into all the world and "punched" in military formation. From now on we shall have to take this spiritual warfare as seriously as we take our military warfare. A new sense of empire will have to get hold of us.

The average Christian in America gives approximately only seven cents a week to foreign missions—a little more than the price of a package of gum! You cannot conquer the world that way! With a national income that had increased to three hundred and eighteen billion dollars in a certain year, spending eighty-one billion dollars for weapons, fifty billion more for luxuries, we gave that same year a billion *less* to churches and to charities, and our gifts for spiritual things were only seventy-three percent of the lowest year of the depression of 1932. This means only one thing: retreat for Christianity if we do not receive this imperialistic passion for the reign of Christ.

> Is this the time to halt, O Church of Christ! to sound
> Retreat? To arm with weapons cheap and blunt,
> The men and women who have borne the brunt
> Of truth's fierce strife, and nobly held their ground?
> Is this the time to halt, when all around
> Horizons lift, new destinies confront,
> Stern duties wait our nation never wont
> To play the laggard, when God's will was found?
> No! Rather strengthen stakes and lengthen cords,
> Enlarge thy plans and gifts, O thou elect,
> And to thy kingdom come for such a time! *

The world is waiting for the sunrise, and Jesus Christ is the Son of God. Would that it could be said everywhere, "The morning light is breaking, the darkness disappears." Was Joshua able to make the sun

* Charles Sumner Hoyt, from *Masterpieces of Religious Verse,* (Harper & Brothers, 1948. Used by permission).

stand still? You and I can, spiritually speaking. We can stand in the way of the "sunrise" or we can bring it to pass.

A soldier lay wounded on a hard-fought field of battle. As the roar of battle died away and in the deathly stillness he lay in the aftermath, across the field there flickered a lantern as survivors were carried away and saved. The poor soldier watched, unable to turn or to speak as the lantern drew near and the surgeon bent over him, examined him and shook his head, saying, "I believe if this fellow lives until sunrise tomorrow he will get well."

All night long the soldier lay with this great hope in his heart and kept saying, "If I live until sunrise, I shall get well." He turned his head to the east to watch for the dawn; at last the stars went out, the east quivered with radiance as the sun rose; his eyes as they followed the orb of day grew brighter as he thought of home, the shady lane, the mossy spring, the wife who had slipped her hand shyly into his own long ago. "I shall look once more," he said, "into her deep, loving eyes." The children would clamor at his knee and little hands would play upon his heartstrings. "If I live until dawning, I shall feel their kisses upon my parched lips and feel their fingers upon my face."

Then the Son of God who died for men, bending down from the stars, put that hand that had been nailed to the cross on the ebbing life and stanched the blood until the stars went out and dawn came. The surgeon came again, and he was taken from death unto life.

The wounded world waits for Christ, but He alone cannot put a hand on the wounded world and stay the flow of blood—not by Himself—for you and I are His hands; you and I are His fingers and if we do not move to bless they pass into sundown without life. They are waiting for the sun—the Son of God, and only you and I can make it rise.

What shall therefore the lord of the vineyard do?

MARK *12:9*

The King Is Here

IT WILL SOON BE CHRISTMAS. BACKGROUND IS NECESSARY for appreciating anything. A jewel is most brilliant in its proper setting and in order to enjoy Christmas, you and I must see it in the setting of the great patience of God. Christmas is the culminating effort of God to win back a sinning world, and it is the conclusion of the greatest love story in history. At Bethlehem that day a King came to be with us. Dig down beneath the foundation of all the debris of happy myth, allegory, parade, tree and tinsel, reindeer and lore, angel and manger, and here is a startling truth, the King has come to earth! "They shall call his name Immanuel, . . . God is with us." For the first time God had walked into human history; the supernatural had come into the natural, and heaven had come down to earth. "The Word was made flesh, and dwelt among us."

God's previous efforts to win the world back to

Himself are described to us in this great love story of Mark 12:1-9:

A certain man planted a vineyard, and set a hedge about it, and digged a place for the winevat, and built a tower, and let it out to husbandmen, and went into a far country. And at the season he sent to the husbandmen a servant, that he might receive from the husbandmen of the fruit of the vineyard. And they caught him, and beat him, and sent him away empty. And again he sent unto them another servant; and at him they cast stones, and wounded him in the head, and sent him away shamefully handled. And again he sent another; and him they killed, and many others; beating some, and killing some. Having yet therefore one son, his well-beloved, he sent him also last unto them, saying, They will reverence my son. But those husbandmen said among themselves, This is the heir; come, let us kill him, and the inheritance shall be ours. And they took him, and killed him, and cast him out of the vineyard. What shall therefore the lord of the vineyard do?

Four times God had invited this world back to Himself and four times this world had defied God, broken His commandments and frustrated His plans. The writer of Hebrews describes it for us in the first chapter, "God, who at sundry times and in divers manners spake in time past unto the fathers by the prophets, hath in these last days spoken unto us by his Son."

Look back at these "divers manners" in which in time past God spoke to His world. Here is a picture of

Eden—the first failure of mankind. Man is walking with God in the garden in the cool of the evening and suddenly, with rebellious heart, he sins and revolts, and you see a family cringing from the sight of God. You see Cain burying his brother Abel in a shallow grave. Murder! Disobedience! This is the answer to God's goodness, and a tryst is broken with God. This is the first failure of mankind to respond to the love of God. Will God now vindicate Himself?

The office of sacrifices is instituted, and God gives to humanity this symbolism of a contrite heart by which man may come back to God.

Then came Abraham and Israel. Here is a nation that dwells in tents, but they are the recipients of God's goodness; manna and quail in sufficience are their lot. He leads them by a pillar of fire by night and a cloud by day. No father ever coddled a child with more patience and love than God coddled Israel. And what was this nation's answer? A golden calf, licentiousness, and grumbling. For sacrifices they brought the ringstraked cattle, the oxen that could not plow, and the meal that soured, the bread that mildewed, and the smallest grain.

God must be angry now, but He will try still another way.

He will send unto them the prophets. Jeremiah will weep with them. Isaiah will plead with them. Malachi will whip them. Haggai will tell how the faithless may come back to God. Ezekiel will paint pictures for them. But man will kill the prophets, stone them; they will be hunted, haunted, and hounded in the caves of the earth. The altars will be torn down. For still another time God, in divers manners, has tried to win the world, and His love once more has been foiled.

Stop here: "What shall therefore the Lord do?" Shall He strike us now with a hand of iron and crush us like a potter's vessel? Will God wither these little human fists thrust in His face? Is the universe insane? Has God no flash point, no anger? Let us see.

There is a conference in heaven, as recorded in Hebrews 10: Christ is saying to God, "Father, the blood of bulls and goats thou dost not desire. A body thou hast prepared me. Lo, I go to do thy will." I see the portals of heaven open. The armies that have guarded the Son of God step back, the portals close behind Him and the hosts are silent. The Prince of Heaven has gone, the right hand at the throne is empty and God's heart is aching. Out of the ivory palaces into a world of woe! Only a great eternal love could make my Saviour go! The star is in the sky at Bethlehem, "For God so loved the world that he gave his only begotten Son." It is Christmas now and God has said, "I will send my well-beloved," and He sent Him also last unto them, saying, "They will reverence my son." But those husbandmen said among themselves, This is the heir; come, let us kill him, and the inheritance shall be ours. And they took him, and killed him, and cast him out of the vineyard. He came to Bethlehem but there was no room for Him in the inn. They scoffed at Him in his boyhood town of Nazareth; they gnashed upon Him with their teeth; some followed Him, to be sure, but He became the object of the most unjust trial in history. They scourged the King's Son, they whipped Him, they squeezed His arteries dry on a cross and laid Him in a borrowed tomb.

Dear God, what wilt Thou do with us now? "What therefore shall the Lord of the vineyard do?"

The answer—God comes to us one Christmas after another in the long-suffering of God! Someone has said there is as much difference between genuine patience and sullen endurance as between the smile of love and the gnashing of teeth. Christmas is God's last plea with the human race. He has sent to us His only begotten Son, there is nothing more that He can do, nothing further is in His plans but repeated presentations of His love, His forgiveness and His program, through His Son, the King of kings; this is the *ne plus ultra* of the heart of God; no other gesture is left!

Still, God, the great Husbandman, digs about the vineyard of the nation; He tills the ground. He has given to America a larger income than ever before in history; we have had parental care from the cradle until now; we learn early the art of prayer—if we wish to learn it; we turn our eyes to the sunrise of prosperity; we have the Bible to light our path as a lamp for our feet; we know as much about God as we wish to know; He gives us strength for our labor, the answers for the questions of our souls, the mercy seat to which we may bring our sins, the glory of a long look even past Easter, the forgiveness of every sin, grace enough for any temptation we wanted to overcome. What more could the Owner of the vineyard do? For myself, I cry back to God, "Thou couldst do nothing more!"

What has Christmas to offer us? Amid all the toys, trinkets, and commercialization of the hour let us keep it a spiritual *holy day* rather than a *holiday*. A girl gazing into a department store window suddenly heard above her a loud speaker playing "Holy Night, Silent Night." With a grimace she scornfully said, "Imagine dragging religion into Christmas!"

How we need all that which religion can give us in this day! Christ came to give us three things.

First of all, He gives us *pardon*. How men have wanted this freedom, pardon from their iniquities! The inadequacy of sacrifices had proven itself; the varied specious excuses that men had conjured up had proven to be shallow defense for their misdeeds; conscience was still alive, and Paul greeted Christmas with these words, "Once in the end of the world hath he appeared to put away sin by the sacrifice of himself in his death."

Here was a new and living way of man's liberation from his transgressions. If Christmas is all that it should mean to you and to me every heart may cry in the acceptance of this salvation, "Unto you is born this day in the city of David a *Saviour,* which is Christ the Lord."

> My sin, O the bliss of that glorious thought,
> My sin—not in part but the whole—
> Is nailed to the cross and I bear it no more,
> Praise the Lord, O my soul.*

Christ came also to give us a *program*. We must bring this world back to God again and place it in the hand of God where it belongs with all its powers, possessions and persons.

We must not satisfy ourselves with being sentimental at Christmas. As James S. Stewart said in one of his works, "There is a type of religion that accepts the consolations of religion without the duties of religion and thus we become sentimental followers of Jesus Christ. Sentimentalism is enjoyment without obligation."** So many would like to enjoy Christ without being obligated to Him. This is impossible.

But when you and I find the comfort of God, we also find the commission of God to service. The dis-

* Christian Service Songs.
** *A Man in Christ.*

covery of Jesus Christ as Lord and Saviour is like the wind filling the sails of a boat, it pushes us on and enables us to carry the cargo of the Spirit. It is like the gift of a job to a man who has long been out of work. It is like giving a man a map when he has lost his way and thereafter he walks in that way. It is not merely offering a man a seat, it is giving him a task to do. You and I would fail miserably to appreciate Christmas unless we have brought to Christ the gifts of the gold of our worship, the frankincense of our possessions, and the myrrh of our service.

Finally, Christ came, not only to bring us His pardon and a program, but also to bring us His Presence. "They shall call his name Immanuel, which, being interpreted, is, God is with us." Christ said, "Lo, I am with you always, even unto the end of the world." One of the greatest fears of mankind is the fear of being alone, and there is no terror that strikes the heart of a man like the terror of not being able to find God or, having found Him, to have lost Him.

I remember one clergyman telling the story of how, during his student days, he sold aluminum that he might earn money for his academic pursuits. One day as he was doing a certain town, with his aluminum samples under his arm, he approached a door, his hand trembling from fright. As he tried to ring the doorbell he could scarcely press it. Suddenly the door opened and there stood the biggest woman he had ever seen!

In total fright and confusion he stammered, "Ma—Ma —Madam, you don't want any aluminum, do you?" She said, "Certainly not. I cannot be bothered," and slammed the door. He went away frightened, conquered, beaten for the day. In his hotel room that evening, he said to the veteran salesman with whom he was canvassing the town, "I can't go through with this." The salesman smiled and said, "I know what is the trouble with you. Tomorrow I will do the other side of the street and just before you ring a doorbell, look over at me and I will salute you this way, and you will know that I am with you." The next day the student went to another door and his knees began to tremble; then, remembering the admonition of his friend, he looked across the way and there he was. He waved to his friend and suddenly a new confidence came over him; he was not alone! He rang the bell and the door opened and there stood the smallest woman he had ever seen! "Madam, I know you would like to look at some aluminum, wouldn't you?" "Certainly," she said. He stepped in. It was a great day. That evening at the hotel, the veteran salesman said to him, "You know, son, the only thing you needed was the power of a presence—to know that you were not alone." How you and I need that!

Frightened hearts we are, in a confused world. Then call His name Jesus, Immanuel, God is with us. You want that, my friends, and so do I. There in the

147

foxholes you can have it, there in the cockpit of a plane, in the hold of a ship; there in the office, in the busy mart, amid the duties of your home, by the clicking typewriter, by the hospital bed, in the valleys of the shadow. When you are all alone and forsaken He can people your heart with a crowd; in the lonely places you can feel the majesty of His presence. At the operating table, in the kitchen, by the crib, and at the governor's desk with its polished power, there He is or may be. Let your heart cry to Him, "O come to us, abide with us, Our Lord Immanuel," and He will come with healing in His wings and you can walk with him forever—and what a walk it will be! That is Christmas, too—the utter fearlessness of a Presence—the King is here!

Then shall the King say unto them on his right hand, Come, ye blessed of my Father, inherit the kingdom prepared for you from the foundation of the world.

MATTHEW *25:34*

Thine Is the Kingdom

Now, THERE IS A STARTLING CONCLUSION TO YOUR LIFE and mine—inheriting a kingdom!

But before we come to this glorious, possible conclusion, let us give our minds and hearts to another startling consideration. The Bible seems full of unusual paradoxes and this one is outstanding—the way in which God chooses to maneuver Himself into a position of seeming helplessness without you and me. In Matthew 21:3 are these arresting words: "The Lord hath need of them." Imagine that! The Creator of the whole universe needing us and what we have! The King of kings standing at the door of your heart and knocking, while the gates of heaven swing open only at His bidding. The Commander of the universe with countless legions at His bidding pleading with us for our meager service! God, the Judge of all the earth, a tender Father pleading with His children. The great illimitable Creator of the world needing His creatures.

Christ, the Heir and Prince of Heaven, yet with no place to lay His head. God, of almighty power, frankly admitting His embarrassment if we do not faithfully serve Him. All this should give thrilling tone to your life and mine.

Jesus said, "I am the vine, ye are the branches. . . . without me ye can do nothing." That is evident, for no branch can bear fruit without the vine. But you remember the complementary truth, do you not? It is this: that any vine is useless without the branches. There are some things that God simply does not choose to do unless He does them through you and me.

Christ said, "I will build my church." We were made to understand that the church was a building and that you and I were the lively stones—the spiritual material—and unless He is able to use us, there is no church. The Church is the body of Christ, He is at its Head, and the mind does not accomplish anything unless the members of that body follow the dictates of the mind, and so God accomplishes little in this universe, in a spiritual way, without our sturdy co-operation.

Why did God run this "holy risk" of placing the Kingdom in the hands of such as us? Why did He not leave it to His miracles instead of to men? Why did He not count on the wonders of His hands instead of on women consecrated to Him? Why did He not use creatures who would have to do His bidding without stubborn delay? Well, there are certain great reasons why God placed the Kingdom in your hand and mine.

First of all, there was *our character*. We are made "in the image of God." We are the only ones who have the capacity for understanding what He wishes to have done. We are the only proper vehicles for this sort of service. An ox may draw a load, but it cannot lift a spiritual burden; a sheep can give wool, but it cannot pray nor commune with God. Someone has suggested that even the angels, unfallen beings, are not tempted in all points like as we are. Neither have they suffered bereavement, nor are their eyes wet with tears, neither have they ever been in hunger. You and I go through these experiences, and, consequently, can reach out and minister to those who know them as we know them.

Then, again, He desires that you and I should build His Kingdom that we might enjoy the *luxury of being used*. Something happens to us spiritually when we are not at the service of God. Religion, you know, is like a hole in your pocket—the more you give away the larger it becomes. The rubber on a tire rots more from disuse than from use. The sponge hardens into rock unless it is squeezed constantly and is relieved of its liquid. A well that is not constantly drawn from becomes stagnant and impossible of use. It is that shorn sheep that is the healthy sheep.

The mechanic in building an engine must allow not only for the intake and combustion, he must also allow for the outgo and the exhaust, otherwise the engine would be blasted to pieces. When God created you and me, He created us spiritually, not only for the intake of His love, goodness, peace, forgiveness and power, but also planned for the outgo, which is our service and the giving-out of ourselves.

Two things are very necessary if our lives are to meet His demands: first, pardon and cleansing—to which end He is our personal Saviour. Second, there is wholehearted service—to which end He is our Lord and Master. If someone asked you to define your religion in one brief sentence, what would you say? Would you accept these words of James in his epistle, 1:27, "Pure religion and undefiled before God and the Father is this, To visit the fatherless and widows in their affliction, and to keep himself unspotted from the world"? Two things are there. One is cleanliness—to keep oneself "unspotted from the world." That is the cross of Christ, His pardon, His redemption, His forgiveness, His cleansing. That is being clean. But it goes on to say, "to visit the fatherless and widows in their affliction,"—that is your cross of service that you must carry. This is *your* part. To keep unspotted from the world is *cleanliness;* to visit the fatherless and the widows in their affliction is *kindness.* You must have both. Some people are kind, but not clean; others are clean, but not kind. These are the right and left wings of an airplane, without both of which we crash to the ground in utter failure. Salvation is to the end of service; we are saved to serve.

We have very little confidence in any religious experience that does not end in an expedition; in any communion with God that does not give itself to a commission; in any type of worship that does not finally consummate itself in spiritual work. To "seek first the kingdom of God, and his righteousness"—to this cause were we born!

A fanatic is a man who redoubles his energies when he has forgotten his aim—and the world is full of fanatics.

It is no little gift to us from God that He has explained to us why we are here—to build a kingdom.

With this comes the *joy of a royal partnership with God.* "How shall two walk together unless they be agreed?" You and I cannot walk with Christ unless we are doing what He is doing—unless we have His purposes and His aims.

One woman said, "Jesus Christ irritates me—He spent his time going around doing good, while I spend my time merely going about." Well, women like that never walk with Christ—they are simply not agreed on what life is all about. Are you? You are here on kingly business.

May I remind you, also, of the *thrill of a confidence* we have in this Kingdom. Someone has suggested that to look around at this world with its chaos and frustration and war, and to believe that God still rules it—that is faith in long trousers, all else is faith in knickerbockers! How true that is. Let us remember that, in spite of all the seeming setbacks of the plan of God in the extension of His kingdom.

When Christ stood there bound with the hempen cords of hatred before Herod, Cæsar's satellite, it seemed that His kingdom did not have the ghost of a chance, but today where are the people who are hotly for Cæsar or hotly against him? Yet Jesus Christ is very much alive. Paul seemed to have little chance against Nero in those Roman days, but who follows Nero now? But how many follow the teachings of Paul! When Hitler exclaimed to Raschnung, "I will tear up the Christian Church by the roots!" how little did he know how impossible it would be to find the roots. As he persecuted the Church, he merely pruned it that it might bear more fruit. There are times in winter when the pruned grape vines look as though they had been stricken with death, but come spring, and they will be filled with purple clusters of luscious grapes. The husbandmen know their business, so does God—the great Husbandman of this universe. Men who try to mutilate the Church only "prune" it so that it may bear more fruit. Jesus Christ has outlived all the dictators who ever marched against Him, and He will. Let us not forget that the last maps will always be made in heaven. You who serve Jesus Christ serve not One who is merely "Christus Consolator"—one who consoles us in our defeats. We also salute and worship "Christus Consummator"—the One who will consummate and finish what He has begun. There is no defeat with Jesus of Nazareth. His Kingdom shall spread from shore to shore, and happy are you, my friends if you have a part in this one deathless movement and fellowship of history.

Then, too, there is the glory of *the final kingdom reward*. I see a picture. One sits upon the throne and on His vestments are written the words, "King of kings and Lord of lords." Angels line the way, myriads stand in the glory of His final empire, and the Church is there, radiant and victorious!

Now I hear a cry which the myriad hosts direct toward Him and these are the words, "Rejoice, for the kingdom of this world has become the kingdom of the Lord and of his Christ, and he shall reign for ever and ever. Hallelujah." It is this that we shall cry to Him.

But may I also ask you to be attentive now, as certain words fall from His kingly lips. Directed to you and to me, and to all of His faithful followers, they are these, "Come, ye blessed of my Father, inherit the kingdom prepared for you from the foundation of the world." Quietly now, majestically now, we see the reason why He has run the holy risk of allowing the whole kingdom to be in the hands of such as you and I. You see, the Kingdom could never belong to us until first we belonged to the Kingdom.

To be sure, in winning men to Himself, God could have splashed with majestic and miraculous hand on the walls of history the words, "Mene, mene, tekel upharsin"—"Thou art weighed in the balances and art found wanting." And thus He could have startled men into an acceptance of His way, but He left it to you and me, by private conversation and personal interviews, to do this so that in the end those souls would not only be His but ours as well.

In that financial campaign in the church or community of which you were a part He could have once more seen to it that coins were picked up from fishes' mouths, and sumptuous golden coins, too, with little effort to those who name His name; but, no, He calls you to sit about His planning tables to fashion that letter that should startle the heart awake with a sense of stewardship.

He might have dropped manna from heaven on the poor, but He chose rather that you visit the sick and the orphaned and the afflicted, and go to the poor with your basket under your arm, with your check made out, remembering that you needed the poor more than they needed you. You saved them from physical starvation, but they saved you spiritually from the death of selfishness.

He could have worked miracles in the missionary

158

enterprise but you women sat down and plotted and planned for a great world-wide kingdom. You plotted and prayed to move hearts and give them a sense of empire, and you it was who splashed His Kingdom across the maps of the world until they were printed in the tricolors of the King of kings.

He could have smitten the enemy with the might of His sword and with the breath of His mouth, but, one by one, you lads give yourselves upon the field of battle, or are willing to do so, in order that in the end you could say to your sons and to God, "I helped the morning break."

You see, my friends, the only way He could exalt you was first to use you; the only way to make the Kingdom belong to you was to see that you first belonged to the Kingdom, and the only way you could be possessors of the Empire of Christ was through the fact that first the Empire of Christ possessed you. Thus on your ears some day, faithful ones, will fall these words, "Come, ye blessed of my Father, inherit the kingdom prepared for you from the foundation of the world."

We invite you into this Kingdom today—to rivet your talents to the things that abide forever, to accept for yourself this purpose of your day.